Sue Hunt

House Party

Coordinated Quilts and Pillows

Martingale®
& COMPANY

House Party:
Coordinated Quilts and Pillows
© 2010 by Sue Hunt

That Patchwork Place® is an imprint of
Martingale & Company®.

Martingale & Company
20205 144th Ave. NE
Woodinville, WA 98072-8478 USA
www.martingale-pub.com

Printed in China
15 14 13 12 11 10   8 7 6 5 4 3 2 1

Library of Congress Cataloging-in-
Publication Data is available upon request.

ISBN: 978-1-56477-999-1

Mission Statement

Dedicated to providing quality products
and service to inspire creativity.

Credits

President & CEO: Tom Wierzbicki
Editor in Chief: Mary V. Green
Managing Editor: Tina Cook
Developmental Editor: Karen Costello Soltys
Technical Editor: Laurie Baker
Copy Editor: Sheila Chapman Ryan
Design Director: Stan Green
Production Manager: Regina Girard
Illustrator: Laurel Strand
Cover & Text Designer: Adrienne Smitke
Photographer: Brent Kane

Dedication

Many thanks to:

My parents, Don and Mariyln Locke (both quilters), for knowing I could do this book and for quilting all the wall hangings in it.

My daughters, Alyssa and Amanda, who always encourage me and have faith in me.

My husband, Joel, for opportunities.

My quilting friends in Japan who always asked me, "When are you going to write a book?"

Contents

23

27

36

39

45

47

55

58

62

65

70

73

Introduction

|||||||||||||||||||||||||||||||||||||||||||||||||||||||||||||||

I often enjoy making a small, quick project between more time-consuming large quilts. Some of my favorite small projects are seasonally themed pillow covers that I rotate throughout the year onto the same pillow form. This allows me to easily create a fresh look on my sofa as the seasons change, and it also saves on storage space. I also enjoy these mostly hand-stitched projects because they're a great take-along size.

In this book, I offer you six seasonal pillow designs, along with a companion quilt project for each of them. The quilts are also small enough for take-along projects and can be completed in a short amount of time. Although they're often referred to as wall hangings, don't let that term limit them to the walls. Small quilts look great draped over a chair or the back of a couch. Try one as a table topper or at the foot of a bed. For the pillows, purchase one 16" pillow form for all the pillow covers. Pillow forms can be found at fabric shops and bed-linen stores.

You will find that the projects offer a variety of techniques that quilters of all levels, from beginner to experienced, can learn from and enjoy. Personally, I like handwork, so I've used hand-stitching techniques in many of the projects. If you don't normally appliqué or quilt by hand, I hope these projects will inspire you to give it a try. Handwork can be relaxing, rewarding, and it's portable! Please, though, don't think that these projects have to be made by hand; they're small enough to lend themselves well to machine stitching. Machine stitching will be necessary for foundation-pieced projects such as "Snowflakes" (page 21) and "Spring Baskets" (page 43), and also the raw-edge appliqué technique used in "Hot!" (page 61). In addition to these techniques, you'll also use rotary-cutting and precision-piecing techniques, and learn to make bias strips, mitered corners, piping, and easy covered buttons.

I hope you'll enjoy starting your own seasonal pillow-and-quilt-partners collection. And don't forget a special friend or family member; these projects make very special gifts, too.

6

Quiltmaking Basics

While it's not possible to cover all quiltmaking techniques in the scope of this book, I have provided information on the special techniques I used to make the projects, such as foundation piecing and freezer-paper appliqué. If you're new to these techniques or need a bit of a refresher, you'll find what you need here.

PRESSING

Machine-sewn seam allowances can either be pressed open or to one side. Often a pressing decision made early on turns out to be incorrect when piecing a later step or even when quilting. The instructions in this book will tell which way seam allowances should be pressed for best results. No matter which way you ultimately press the seam allowances, begin by lightly pressing over the seam as it was sewn. This quick press smoothes the stitches and the fabric.

Seam allowances open. Some seam allowances work better when pressed open. Pressing seam allowances open helps distribute the bulk between blocks and rows. It also prevents the potential mistake of pressing a one-way seam allowance the wrong way, which could create a very bulky intersection.

From the wrong side of the fabric, gently open the seam allowances with the tip of the iron (you may need to use your fingers to get it started). Lightly press the seam allowances open. Turn the piece to the right side of the fabric and press again, wiggling the iron back and forth a bit over the seam and applying more pressure. Make sure the seam allowances are flat and that there are no tucks in the fabric.

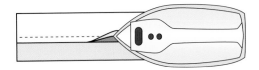

Seam allowances to one side. Lay the piece closed, with the fabric the seam will be pressed toward facing up. For example, if you have sewn a light fabric and a dark fabric together and you will be pressing toward the dark fabric, place the pieces on your ironing surface with the dark fabric facing up. Place the tip of the iron between the two pieces of fabric (the right sides of the fabrics) and move it toward the seam. Press away from you, gently smoothing over the seam with the iron tip. When the seam allowances are flat with no tucks in the seam, press with more pressure.

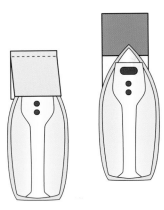

FOUNDATION PIECING

In foundation piecing, the pattern is drawn onto paper, and then the fabric is sewn directly to the paper, which is later removed. This method provides a greater accuracy for intricate designs with points, like "Snowflakes" (page 21), or provides stability and guidelines to follow for designs such as "Spring Baskets" (page 43).

Several commercial papers made specifically for foundation piecing are available at quilt shops and online. Most of the papers can be used in a copy machine or printer to transfer the pattern, as well as used for hand tracing. Always check the accuracy of machine-printed patterns because sometimes distortion can occur.

Other types of paper can also be used for your foundations. I've tried several different papers that I've had on hand with mixed results. *Tracing paper* is easy to see through when tracing and sewing, and some tracing papers can be used on copy machines when lots of copies are needed. However, tracing paper can be hard to remove after sewing. *Printer paper* is harder to see through when tracing and sewing, but of course works well in a printer or copy machine for multiple copies. It too is messy and hard to remove after sewing. My favorite on-hand foundation paper so far has been *calligraphy paper*. I prefer the practice type of calligraphy paper rather than the regular art type because it's thinner. It's easier to remove after sewing than tracing and printer paper, but it can't be used in a copy machine or printer. Calligraphy paper can be found at art stores and online.

To foundation piece:

1. Copy the patterns provided with the project onto the desired foundation paper using either a photocopier or a printer, or by hand tracing them. If you're hand tracing, make sure you transfer the number of the piece and the fabric it will be cut from. Be sure to also include the name of each pattern if there is more than one for your project. Make the number of copies indicated in the instructions. You can put more than one pattern on each piece of paper, but leave a little bit of space between each one so that the finished pieces can be trimmed neatly on the outer lines later. To make a reversed pattern, copy one pattern onto foundation paper, and then use a window or light box to help you see through the paper so you can trace it onto the back of the paper. Make sure the pattern is accurate, and then use it to make the rest of the required patterns.

2. Cut out each pattern, leaving a little bit of extra paper around the outside lines of each pattern.

3. Accuracy isn't too important when cutting the fabric for foundation piecing but I find that it's easier to precut the shapes. Make quick paper templates by tracing each numbered area from the foundation pattern onto another piece of paper. Add ¼" seam allowance all around each piece, and then cut them out. *Reversed templates must be made from reversed patterns.* Pin the paper template to the wrong side of the appropriate fabric, making sure it's face

up; trace around the piece. Remove the piece and use it to trace as many additional pieces as necessary. When you have the required amount traced, cut them out. You do not have to be exact when cutting the pieces from fabric but it's better to cut a larger piece than a smaller one. Keep your fabric shapes separated according to the section they will cover on the pattern and label them to avoid confusion.

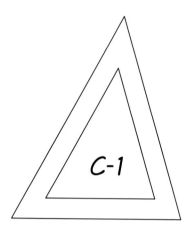

Paper template from
Snowflake C pattern

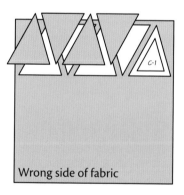

Wrong side of fabric

4. Hold the pattern up to a window or light source so you can see through it and so that the marked side is facing you. Place the fabric shape for section 1 behind section 1 so that the wrong side of the fabric is facing the paper. Make sure there is at least ¼" of fabric extending beyond all of the section-1 lines. Lay the fabric shape for section 2 over section 2 in the same manner, and then carefully flip it onto the section-1 fabric so they're right sides together. Pin the pieces in place at right angles to the seam between sections 1 and 2. Sew on the line between sections 1 and 2, beginning and ending

one or two stitches before and after the line. *Do not backstitch.* Trim the seam allowance to ⅛". Press the fabric 2 piece to the right side. Make sure section 2 is completely covered and there is at least ¼" extra on all the unstitched sides.

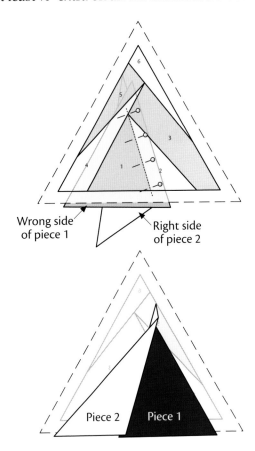

Wrong side of piece 1

Right side of piece 2

Piece 2   Piece 1

5. Continue adding the fabric pieces in numerical order until all of the pieces have been added. When all of the pieces have been added, trim along the outer line of the pattern.
6. Remove the paper when instructed for each project.

MAKING TEMPLATES

Some of the pieces for "Umbrellas" (page 33), "Spring Baskets" (page 43), and "Hot!" (page 61) will need to be cut out using templates. Templates can be made from cardboard or heavy paper, but because the edges of these materials wear away and become inaccurate after a few uses, I recommend making your templates from clear template plastic. You can find template plastic at most quilt shops.

To make a template, trace the pattern from the book onto the template plastic. Often there is a rougher side to the plastic that will hold a pencil mark. If not, a fine-line permanent pen usually works. Label the template with the grain line and the name of the piece, and then mark a large "R" on the reverse side of the piece so you will be able to keep track of the right and reverse sides of nonsymmetrical pieces. Cut out the template on the outer drawn line, which is the seam line. The templates in this book do not include a seam allowance.

To use a template, place the fabric wrong side up on a board covered with fine-grit sandpaper. Place the template on the correct grain line of the fabric and accurately draw around it. Draw another line ¼" from the first line for the seam allowance. Cut out the fabric shape on the outer line.

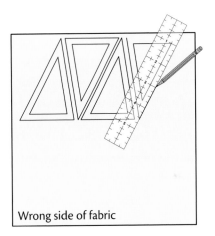

Wrong side of fabric

FREEZER-PAPER APPLIQUÉ

While there are several methods of appliqué, my favorite for simple shapes is one that uses freezer-paper patterns. The patterns are easily traced onto the paper from templates and cut out, and then each one is ironed to the wrong side of the appropriate fabrics to serve as a guide for better precision. The freezer-paper method keeps larger pieces flat and the edges of the appliqué shapes smooth and crisp. Freezer paper can be found at grocery stores and some quilt shops.

1. Using the pattern(s) given with the project, trace each appliqué shape onto the non-shiny side of the freezer paper. You will need the number of shapes indicated on the pattern, but

normally each freezer-paper shape can be used more than once. For reversed patterns, trace the pattern onto the shiny side of the paper. Mark the fabric grain lines where indicated. Cut out each shape on the drawn lines.

2. With a dry iron set on the cotton setting, press each freezer-paper shape onto the wrong side of the appropriate fabric, shiny side down and observing the grain line. Leave enough space between the pieces that are cut from the same fabric to allow for a scant ¼" seam allowance around each piece. When pressing, press straight down on the freezer-paper shape first, and then gently move the iron around a little using medium pressure for about 10 seconds. Let the shape cool, and then check to see if the freezer paper is adhered. Loose shapes can be pressed again, even when you're sewing. If the paper refuses to stick to the fabric or it is difficult to remove after sewing, you've pressed too much; cut another shape from freezer paper if needed.

3. Cut out each fabric shape a scant ¼" from the freezer-paper shape. Fold under the seam allowances and gently make a crease with your fingernail at the edge of the paper all around the shape. When all of the seam allowances have been folded under and creased, unfold them.

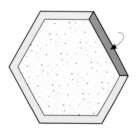

4. Place the prepared piece in the desired location on the quilt top. Pin the shape in place in the seam allowances *only*. Pinning through the freezer paper may cause it to release from the fabric.

5. Using thread that matches the appliqué, blind stitch all but about 1" of the shape to the background, turning the seam allowance under with the needle as you go and using your non-sewing fingers to hold it down. Remove pins as you go along. To eliminate bulk at the right-angle points in the "Fall Walk in the Park" projects,

trim a bit of the corner seam allowance on the diagonal, fold under the diagonal edge, and then fold under the seam allowance on one side of the corner, and finally the seam allowance on the other side of the corner. For the hexagon angles in the "Snowflakes" and "Umbrellas" projects, fold under the seam allowance on one side of the point, and then fold under the seam allowance on the other side of the point.

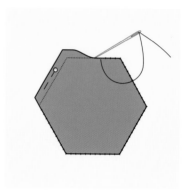

6. Before you stitch all of the edges down, decide how you will remove the freezer-paper shape. There are a couple of different ways you can do this.

   Method 1. Use this method when you don't need to cut away the background fabric behind the appliqué. Start stitching on a straight edge, not at a corner. When you are about 1" or less from finishing, stop sewing, finger-press the remainder of the seam allowance under again, unfold, and remove the shape. To loosen the paper, insert something dull and flat (try a thin crochet hook) between the paper and fabric. Pull out the paper (tweezers may help here) and finish stitching the appliqué in place.

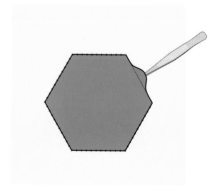

Pull paper through opening.

Method 2. Use this paper-removal method when the background fabric behind the appliqué is to be cut away. Stitch around the entire shape. Carefully cut away the background fabric behind the appliqué shape, leaving a ⅛" to ¼" seam allowance. Remove the freezer-paper shape.

Cut away background fabric
behind appliqué.

BIAS-STRIP APPLIQUÉ

Bias-cut strips are used for the curved appliqué pieces of the pillows and wall hangings in "Spring Baskets" (page 43) and "Summer Flowers" (page 53). Handle bias strips gently so they don't stretch out of shape and distort.

Using your rotary cutter, cut 1"-wide bias strips the length indicated for the project. Fold under ¼" on each long side of each strip and pin or baste the folded edges in place. Iron the folds. Bias-tape makers are available at quilt shops and fabric stores to make this step easier. Pin the strip in place on the quilt top where indicated and hand appliqué the edges.

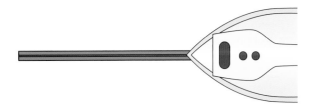

Pillow Construction

The pillow tops in this book were quilted before assembling the pillow, and were embellished with piping and covered buttons. All of the steps to complete the pillows are covered here.

Quilting Your Pillow Top

1. Layer the muslin backing square with the batting square, and then the completed pillow top, right side up. Smooth the layers by hand from the center out first, and then turn them over and smooth from the backing side. Turn the layers back over so the pillow top is facing up.

2. Hand baste the layers together as shown, using a long, thin needle and working from the center out to the edges. Do not trim the excess batting and backing; the extra may come in handy if the top shifts during quilting.

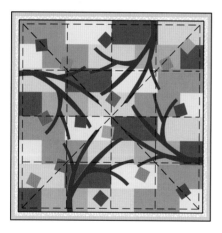

3. Quilt as desired by hand or machine. Quilting patterns or suggestions are given for some of the projects. Because these projects are small, the pillow top can be hand quilted with a small-diameter quilting hoop or without any hoop at all. Always quilt from the center out. The hand-quilting thread tension should be a little looser when not using a hoop.

Making Piping

The piping in this book is made with 1"-wide bias fabric strips and $5/32$"-diameter cotton cording. If you choose a larger cording, you'll need to cut wider bias strips accordingly.

1. Using your rotary cutter, cut 1"-wide bias strips from the piping fabric. Cut enough strips to make at least a 68" length when the strips are sewn together.

2. Join the strips on the angled ends using a ¼" seam allowance. Press the seam allowances open.

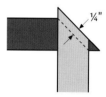

Working the Angles

If the angled ends don't match, lay the two strips to be joined on top of each other, right sides up and long edges aligned. Cut the ends to be joined at an angle with the rotary cutter. It isn't necessary to cut an exact 45° angle; as long as the angles are the same they will join correctly.

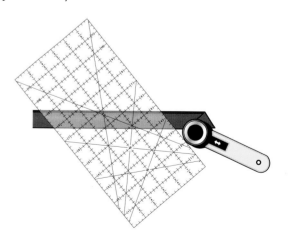

3. Lightly press the strip in half lengthwise, wrong sides together. Open up the strip, lay the cording in the fold, and then bring the strip edges together again so that the cording is enveloped.

4. With the raw edges aligned and using a zipper foot, stitch next to the cording on the strip's right side, but not as close as you can. You will need to sew closer to the cording later.

COVERING BUTTONS

For more interest, use a variety of different-sized round buttons, ⅝" and larger, and cover each with an assortment of the fabrics that were used on the pillow top. The buttons can have shanks or holes. Remember that buttons can be a choking hazard, so they should be omitted on pillows that will be used by young children.

1. Place the button on the wrong side of the desired fabric and draw around it with a sharp pencil. Draw a second circle ⅜" from the first circle. Don't worry about being exactly accurate! Cut out the circle on the outer line.

2. Run a gathering stitch around the edge of the fabric circle, leaving thread tails at the beginning and end. Place the button in the center of the circle and pull on the thread tails to gather the fabric around the button. Tie the ends in a knot to secure.

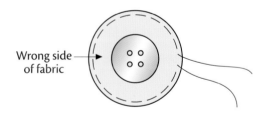
Wrong side of fabric

CONSTRUCTING THE PILLOW BACK

1. With right sides together and using a ¼" seam allowance, sew a 7" x 17" muslin lining piece to a 12" x 17" pillow-back fabric piece along the 17" edges. Press the seam allowances toward the lining piece. Fold the joined piece in half lengthwise to measure 9¼" x 17". Press along

the fold line. Edge stitch 1/16" from the pressed edge. Repeat to make a total of two back pieces.

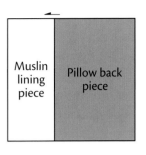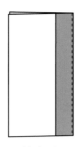
Muslin lining piece · Pillow back piece

Make 2.

2. Set aside one back piece. On the remaining back piece, mark the buttonhole placement. *For three buttonholes*, begin by marking the vertical center of the back piece along the edge-stitched edge. Measure 4" above and below the center mark and make a mark at each point. These will be the center marks for each buttonhole. *For four buttonholes*, make a mark approximately 3⅝" from the top of the back piece along the edge-stitched edge. Measure from this mark approximately 3¼" and make another mark. Continue in this manner to make two additional marks.

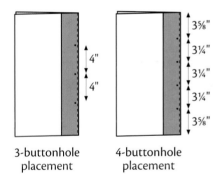
3-buttonhole placement · 4-buttonhole placement
4" · 4" · 3⅝" · 3¼" · 3¼" · 3¼" · 3⅝"

3. Insert small scraps of lightweight fusible interfacing or leftover back fabric between the layers of the back piece next to the fold and under where each buttonhole will be made; pin them in place.

4. Measure the buttons and draw the buttonhole length needed on the back piece, centering the buttonhole over each mark and placing them parallel and ½" from the edge-stitched edge. Make the buttonholes by hand or machine. Press the piece.

5. Trim both back pieces to 9" x 16½".

ASSEMBLING THE PILLOW

1. Remove all of the quilting marks and basting threads from the pillow top; press (make sure all marks are removed and take care to not iron directly on any polyester batting).

2. Use a rotary cutter and ruler to trim the top to 16½" square. In some cases the quilting will pull the top in too much and a 16½" square isn't possible. If this happens, trim the quilted pillow top so it's square and as large as possible. Fortunately pillow forms have give in them and will fit a slightly smaller pillow cover. If the top is cut smaller, adjust the pillow back pieces to fit the new size, trimming from the 16½" dimension, not the 9".

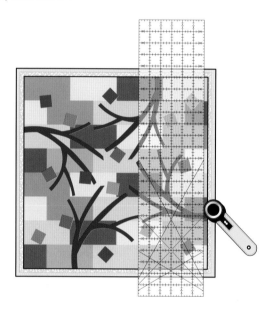

3. Sew the piping around the edge of the pillow top. With the raw edges aligned, lay the piping on the right side of the trimmed pillow top, beginning approximately 3" from a corner. Using a zipper foot, begin sewing about 1" away from the beginning of the piping. Sew very close to the cording. As you approach each corner, make four or five clips in the piping seam allowance just to the previous line of stitching on the piping. Bend the piping around the corner of the pillow top and pin it in place. Slowly stitch around the slightly rounded corners and continue stitching. As you reach the end, angle the piping ends off the pillow edges

and continue sewing over them in the same seam line. Trim off the excess piping.

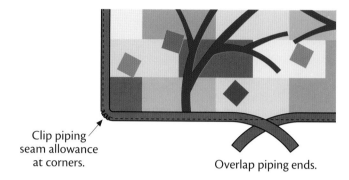

Clip piping seam allowance at corners.

Overlap piping ends.

4. With right sides together and raw edges aligned, place the back piece with the buttonholes over one half of the pillow top. The finished edge will be near the pillow center. Place the remaining back piece over the other half of the pillow top, overlapping the buttonhole back approximately 1¼" at the pillow center. Pin the pieces in place. Sew around the pillow using a zipper foot and sewing as close as possible to the cord in the piping. Trim the seam allowance diagonally at each corner. Turn the pillow inside out through the opening in the back. Check that the stitching next to the piping doesn't show. If it does show, re-sew these areas.

1¼" overlap

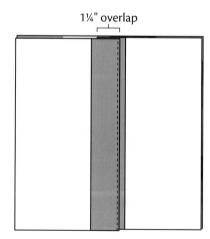

5. Sew the covered buttons to the non-buttonhole back piece to correspond to the buttonhole locations, sewing through the fabric covering the button if you did not cover a shank button. On two- or four-hole buttons, use embroidery thread in a contrasting color for more interest, if desired. You might also try a cross stitch or other design when attaching four-hole buttons.

From sewing accurate borders to attaching binding to adding a hanging sleeve, here you'll find what you need to finish your quilt.

ADDING BORDERS

Not all of the projects have borders, but those that do will either be pieced or have mitered corners, and in some instances there will be a pieced border with mitered corners. The cutting instructions for each project will indicate the dimensions to cut the border strips. Extra length and width are allowed for size variations and for squaring up the quilt later. The instructions for pieced borders are given with the individual project. Follow the instructions here for borders with mitered corners.

1. Measure both side edges of the quilt top. If the measurements are not the same, determine the average. Divide this number in half and make a note of the measurement. Repeat with the top and bottom edges of the quilt top.

2. Fold each border strip in half and mark the center with a pin. Using the results of the side measurement from step 1 (the half length), on two border strips, measure that distance from the pin in both directions and place another pin. Repeat with the remaining two border strips using the top and bottom half-width measurement.

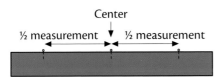

Center

½ measurement ½ measurement

3. Fold the quilt in half lengthwise and mark the center of the top and bottom edges with a pin. Fold the quilt in half widthwise and mark the center of each side edge with a pin.

4. With right sides together and raw edges aligned, pin a side border strip to the side of the quilt top, matching the center pin marks first, and then matching the remaining pins on the border strip with the top and bottom edges of the quilt. Add additional pins in the space between the pins to secure the strips. Small amounts of excess can be eased when stitching.

5. Beginning and ending ¼" from the corners of the quilt top, stitch the border strip in place, backstitching at the beginning and end and easing as necessary. Press the seam allowances toward the border. Repeat with the remaining border strips (it does not matter which order you sew on the strips).

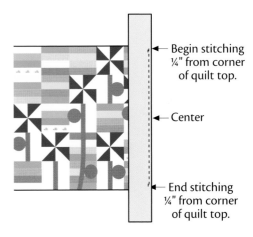

Begin stitching ¼" from corner of quilt top.

Center

End stitching ¼" from corner of quilt top.

6. Lay the first corner to be mitered on your ironing board with the main part of the quilt to the left and below the corner. Fold the top border strip up and under to form a right angle at the corner. Temporarily flip the seam allowances of the right-hand border strip toward the quilt, and then position the border strip under the top border strip. Check to make sure the folded strip is at a 45° angle, and then press the fold. Place a few pins in the border strips where the excess overlaps above the corner.

7. Carefully fold the quilt top in half diagonally, right sides together, so the top border is on top of and aligned with the right-hand border. Pin along the pressed-in line. If the crease isn't very visible, draw over it with pencil or chalk before pinning.

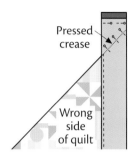

Pressed crease

Wrong side of quilt

8. Backstitching at the beginning and end, stitch on the crease, sewing from the quilt corner to the border outer edge. Remove the pins and take the piece back to the ironing board. Open up the quilt and make sure the seam lies flat and that the angle is good. Flip the right-hand border seam allowances back toward the border. Open the mitered seam and press from the front of the quilt, and then turn the quilt over and trim the mitered seam allowance to ¼".

9. Repeat steps 6–8 with the remaining three corners.

QUILTING YOUR WALL HANGING

Layer the quilt top with batting and backing in the same manner as for pillows (see "Quilting Your Pillow Top" on page 14). Baste, if needed, as shown below. Most of the projects in this book have been hand quilted, but that's not to say that you couldn't quilt them by machine or have your favorite long-arm machine quilter finish them for you. Some of the patterns include quilting suggestions based on the designs I used on the projects.

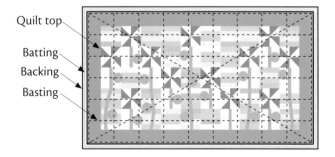

Quilt top

Batting

Backing

Basting

MAKING AND ATTACHING BINDING

Cut your binding strips across the width of the fabric (from selvage to selvage) rather than the length of the fabric so they have a little bit of stretch. I find that binding strips cut 1¾" wide make a nice, tight finished binding when using lightweight batting, but if you want more ease or are using a thicker batting, cut your binding strips 2" to 2½" wide.

1. With right sides together, join the strips with a diagonal seam. Trim the seam allowances to ¼" and press them open.

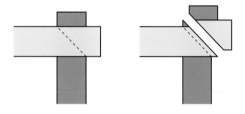

2. Trim one end of the joined strip at a 45° angle. Press under the angled end ¼". Fold the strip in half lengthwise, wrong sides together, and press.

Fold line

3. Remove all of the quilting marks and basting threads on your quilt, and then lay it on your cutting table with a rotary-cutting mat under one corner. Use a rotary-cutting ruler and cutter to square up the corner and edges, cutting the excess batting and backing even with the quilt top (refer to step 2 of "Assembling the Pillow" on page 16). In some projects the border width is wider than necessary to allow for trimming the edges to square up the quilt. Compare opposite sides with each other and make minor adjustments to make them the same length.

4. With the raw edges aligned, place the binding on the front of the quilt, with the end of the binding about 6" from a corner. Sew the binding in place using a ¼" seam allowance and beginning about 3" from the angled end of the

binding with a backstitch. Stop sewing ¼" from the first corner; backstitch.

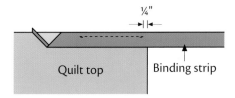

Quilt top Binding strip

5. Remove the quilt from the sewing machine. Fold up the binding at a 90° angle, then down again so the edge of the binding is even with the edge of the quilt. Start sewing at the fold of the binding and stop sewing ¼" from the next corner. Repeat with the remaining corners.

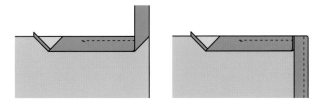

6. When you're about 3" from the beginning of the binding, stop sewing and backstitch. Remove the quilt from the machine. Trim the end of the binding so it overlaps the beginning about ½". Tuck the end inside the beginning and pin it in place. Finish sewing the seam.

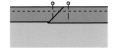

7. Turn the binding to the back of the quilt and hand stitch it in place, mitering the corners and stitching the angled edge of the binding together where the ends are joined.
8. Attach a hanging sleeve and label, if desired.

ADDING A HANGING SLEEVE

Because these wall hangings are small and light-weight, a narrow dowel rod is sufficient to hold them up. A fabric sleeve is used to hold the dowel rod in place. The sleeve fabric can be the same fabric as the backing, a coordinating fabric, or just a piece of muslin. The materials list for each project in the book allows for extra backing yardage to be used for the sleeve.

1. Cut a strip of fabric 5" wide and the width of the quilt.
2. Turn under one short end ¼" twice and machine stitch the hem in place. Fold the strip in half lengthwise, *wrong* sides together, and stitch the long edges together using a ¼" seam allowance. Press the tube flat, with the seam positioned in the center and the seam allowances pressed open.

3. With the seam facing the quilt backing, pin the sleeve to the quilt back, positioning the hemmed end ½" from one side edge and ½" from the top edge. Keeping the sleeve parallel to the top edge, slip-stitch the sleeve in place along the top edge, starting at the hemmed end. Stop sewing 2" from the unfinished end. Trim the raw edge even with the side of the quilt. Turn under the raw edge ¼" twice and hand stitch the hem in place. Keeping the back of the sleeve flat, nudge the bottom pressed edge up about ¼" and pin it in place. This will create extra ease in the sleeve for the rod. Finish sewing along the top edge, then down the edge of the hemmed end against the quilt back, and along the new bottom edge of the sleeve.

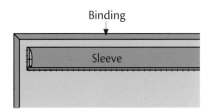

Binding

Sleeve

LABELING YOUR QUILT

It's important to document your work by putting your name, date, and any other pertinent information on the quilt. Most often this is done by attaching a label to the back. I like to embroider my name and the date on the back in addition to adding a label with more information.

Snowflakes

The blue and white fabrics give this pillow-and-wall hanging couple a crisp winter look. Foundation piecing provides the snowflakes with sharp points; easy precision piecing adds interest to the borders.

FINISHED PILLOW: 16" X 16" • FINISHED QUILT: 34¾" X 42"

MATERIALS

Materials listed here are sufficient to make both the wall hanging and the pillow. Yardage is based on 42"-wide fabric.

When choosing the background fabric, look for a non-directional print that isn't too busy. With foundation piecing, the pieces tend to go in different directions, so the effect can be messy if the fabric is too busy. Also, look for a white that is printed with a white pattern. A print offers more interest than a solid, but if you can't find one, a bright solid white works well, too.

For the pillow and wall hanging

3 yards of dark blue fabric for backgrounds, snowflakes, borders, pillow piping, and wall-hanging binding
1⅓ yards of white fabric for snowflakes, sashing, and borders
2⅛ yards of fabric for pillow back, wall-hanging backing, and wall-hanging sleeve
Foundation paper
Freezer paper

For the pillow

¾ yard of lightweight muslin for backing and lining
21" x 21" square of batting
2 yards of ⁵⁄₃₂"-diameter cotton cording
3 assorted-size buttons, ⅝" and larger, to cover
16" pillow form

For the wall hanging

39" x 46" piece of batting

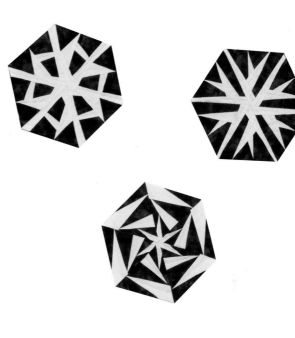

CUTTING

All measurements include ¼"-wide seam allowances. Cut all pieces across the width of the fabric unless otherwise noted.

For the pillow and wall hanging

From the *lengthwise grain* of the dark blue fabric, cut:

4 strips, 3" x 22", for pillow
2 strips, 4" x 51", for wall hanging
2 strips, 4" x 41", for wall hanging

From the remaining dark blue fabric, cut:

1 square, 13½" x 13½", for pillow
20 squares, 7½" x 7½", for wall hanging
Enough 1¾"-wide strips to make a 164"-long strip
    when joined end to end, for wall hanging

From the *bias* of the remaining dark blue fabric, cut:

Enough 1"-wide strips to make a 68"-long strip
    when joined end to end, for pillow
Set aside the remaining fabric for paper piecing.

From the *lengthwise grain* of the white fabric, cut:

14 strips, ¾" x 40"; crosscut into 4 strips, ¾" x 29¼",
    and 15 strips, ¾" x 7½". Set aside the remaining
    strips for the pillow and wall-hanging borders.
Set aside the remaining fabric for paper piecing.

From the fabric for pillow back and wall-hanging backing, cut:

2 pieces, 12" x 17", for pillow
1 piece, 39" x 46", for wall hanging
Set aside the remaining fabric for making a wall-
    hanging sleeve, if desired.

For the pillow

From the muslin, cut:

1 square, 21" x 21"
2 rectangles, 7" x 17"

Pillow

FOUNDATION PIECING
THE SNOWFLAKES

1. Select three snowflake foundation patterns from patterns A–E (pages 29–31). Refer to "Foundation Piecing"(page 9) to make six of each foundation (you need six to make one snowflake). If you're hand tracing, be sure to transfer the numbers and fabrics for each section and mark the center on each pattern.

2. Foundation piece all six foundations for one snowflake using the remaining dark blue and white fabrics. When all six foundations are finished, press each one flat. Trim on the outer pattern line.

Assembly-Line Sewing

The piecing goes much faster if you add the same piece to each of the six foundations before adding the next. In other words, stitch the 1 and 2 pieces on each pattern, add the 3 piece to each pattern, and so forth.

3. Sew two foundations together, matching the center points and end points. Press the seam allowances open. Sew a third foundation to the pair. Press the seam allowances open. Repeat for the remaining three foundations to make a total of two snowflake halves. Sew the halves

together, paying careful attention to match the center intersection. Press the seam allowances open. Firmly press the entire piece. Remove all of the paper. This can be messy, so plan to vacuum afterward!

4. Repeat steps 2 and 3 with the remaining foundations to make a total of three snowflakes.

MAKING AND ADDING THE BORDER STRIPS

1. About 1" from the center of one dark blue 3" x 22" strip, use a chalk pencil or white removable ink marker to draw an angled line the width of the strip. Make two additional angled lines 2½" to 3" apart on both sides of the first line, making sure your lines stay within the center 13" of the strip (leave about 4½" at each end). The angles can be anywhere from 45° to 90° but should be random and not measured.

2. Cut along one of the marked lines to divide the strip into two pieces. With right sides together, place a white print ¾" x 40" strip on the angled edge of one of the two blue pieces. Sew ¼" from the angled edge. Press the seam allowances toward the blue strip. Trim the white strip

even with the top and bottom edges of the blue piece.

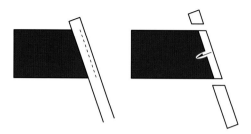

3. Align the angled edge of the remaining blue piece from step 2 with the raw edge of the white strip on the piece from step 2. With the white strip on top, sew ¼" from the *first line of stitching*. Press the seam allowances toward the blue piece.

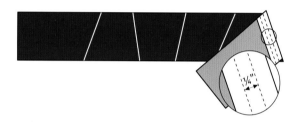

Precision Piecing

Achieving the perfect ¼"-wide white strip is easiest to do if you use a presser foot that measures ¼" from the needle center to both the left and right edges. If you only have one that measures ¼" to the right edge, turn the piece around so the bulk of the fabric is on the right, not the left. Then, sew using the right edge of the presser foot as the guide.

4. Repeat steps 2 and 3 with the remaining marked lines.
5. Repeat steps 1–4 with the remaining three blue 3" x 22" strips and white ¾" x 40" strips.
6. For each border strip, straighten the long edge that will be sewn to the center square. Keep the width consistent for each strip and do not cut

off more than necessary. You'll trim the opposite edge after quilting.

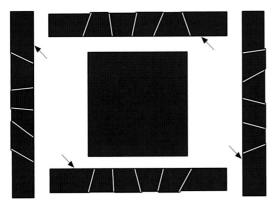

Straighten inner edges.

7. Refer to "Adding Borders" (page 17) to sew the border strips to the 13½" square and miter the corners.

Appliquéing the Snowflakes

1. Referring to "Freezer-Paper Appliqué" (page 11) and using the hexagon appliqué pattern (page 32), trace one hexagon onto the non-shiny side of a piece of freezer paper and cut it out. You'll reuse the freezer-paper template for each snowflake.

2. Center the freezer-paper template, shiny side down, onto the wrong side of a snowflake so that the edges of the snowflake are parallel with the edges of the template. Using an iron, press the template in place. Press the seam allowances of the snowflake over the template.

3. Place the prepared snowflake on the pillow top as desired, referring to the photo if needed. When you're happy with the placement, pin the snowflake in place. Appliqué the snowflake in place and remove the freezer-paper template using method 2.

4. Repeat steps 2 and 3 with the remaining snowflakes.

Finishing the Pillow

Follow the instruction under "Pillow Construction" (page 14) to finish constructing the pillow. Use the snowflake quilting pattern (page 31), if desired, to quilt the pillow top.

Wall Hanging

Foundation Piecing the Snowflakes

1. Using snowflake foundation patterns A–E (pages 29–31), refer to "Foundation Piecing"(page 9) to make six of each foundation (you need six to make one snowflake). If you're hand tracing, be sure to transfer the numbers and fabrics for each section and mark the center on each pattern. Select four of the patterns and make a reversed pattern of each. From each of the reversed patterns, make six foundations. This will give you a total of nine different snowflakes when they're complete.

2. Refer to steps 2 and 3 of "Foundation Piecing the Snowflakes" (page 23) to make a total of nine snowflakes.

Assembling the Wall-Hanging Center

1. Sew a white ¾" x 7½" vertical sashing strip to one side of 15 dark blue 7½" squares, referring to "Precision Piecing" (page 24). Press the seam allowances toward the squares.

2. Sew three squares from step 1 together side by side as shown, again referring to "Precision Piecing" to achieve the ¼"-wide white strip. Add a plain dark blue 7½" square to the end of the row. Press the seam allowances toward the blue squares. Repeat to make a total of five rows.

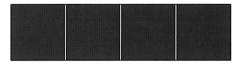

Make 5.

3. Sew a white ¾" x 29¼" horizontal sashing strip to the bottom of four of the rows. Carefully sew using ¼" seam allowances as before. Press the seam allowances toward the blue squares. Sew the rows together with the unsashed row on the bottom.

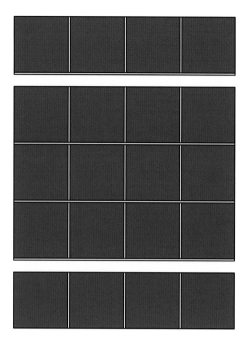

MAKING AND ADDING THE BORDER STRIPS

1. Referring to the pillow instructions for making and adding the border strips (page 24), mark the dark blue 4" x 41" strips with five angled lines. Make the first mark about 3½" from the center of the strip. Mark two additional angled lines 6½" to 7" apart on both sides of the first line, making sure your lines stay within the center 29" of the strip (leave about 6" at each end). Mark the dark blue 4" x 51" strips in the same manner, drawing the first line about 4½" from the center. Make two additional angled lines 8" to 9" apart on both sides of the first line, making sure your lines stay within the center 36" of the border (leave about 7½" at each end). Using the remaining white ¾" x 40" strips, cut one angled line at a time and insert the strip.

2. For each border strip, straighten the long edge that will be sewn to the wall-hanging center. Keep the width consistent for each strip and do not cut off more than necessary. You will trim the opposite edge after quilting.

3. Refer to "Adding Borders" (page 17) to sew the shorter border strips to the top and bottom of the quilt center and the longer border strips to the sides, mitering the corners.

APPLIQUÉING THE SNOWFLAKES

1. Referring to the pillow instructions for appliquéing the snowflakes, use the hexagon appliqué pattern (page 32) to trace three hexagons onto the non-shiny side of a piece of freezer paper and cut them out. You'll reuse the templates.

2. Press the freezer-paper templates onto the wrong side of three snowflakes and place them on the quilt top as desired, referring to the photo if needed. When you're happy with the placement, pin the snowflakes in place. Appliqué the snowflakes in place and remove the freezer-paper templates using method 2. Repeat with the remaining snowflakes using the removed freezer-paper templates.

FINISHING THE WALL HANGING

Refer to "Wall-Hanging Construction" (page 17).
1. Layer the wall-hanging top with batting and backing; baste the layers together.
2. Quilt, referring to the photos (on the previous pages) for ideas and using the snowflake quilting pattern (page 31), if desired. Quilted snowflakes are randomly scattered across the background.
3. The border for this wall hanging was cut oversized; after quilting, trim it to about 3" wide to square up the quilt.
4. Bind the wall hanging using the dark blue 1¾"-wide strips.
5. Add a hanging sleeve and label, if desired.

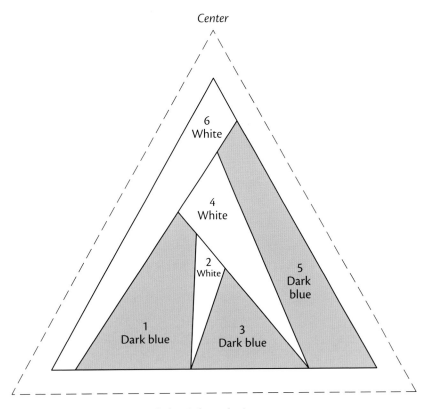

Snowflake A foundation pattern

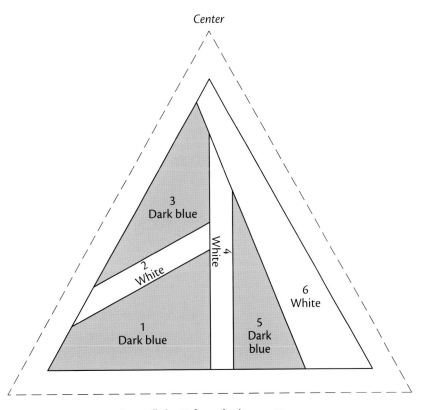

Snowflake B foundation pattern

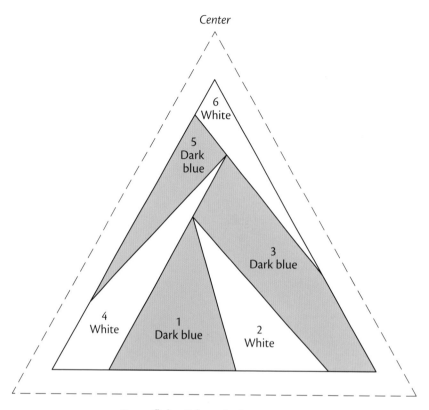

Snowflake C foundation pattern

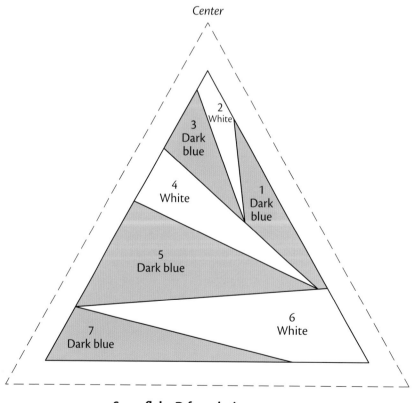

Snowflake D foundation pattern

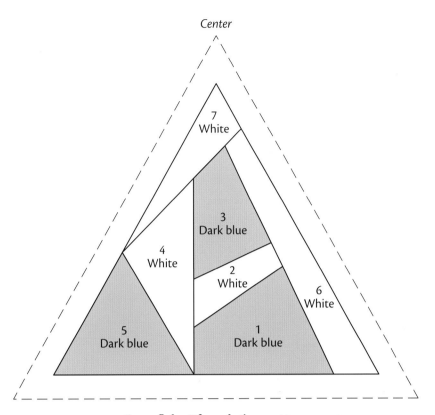

Center

7
White

3
Dark blue

4
White

2
White

6
White

5
Dark blue

1
Dark blue

Snowflake E foundation pattern

Snowflake quilting pattern

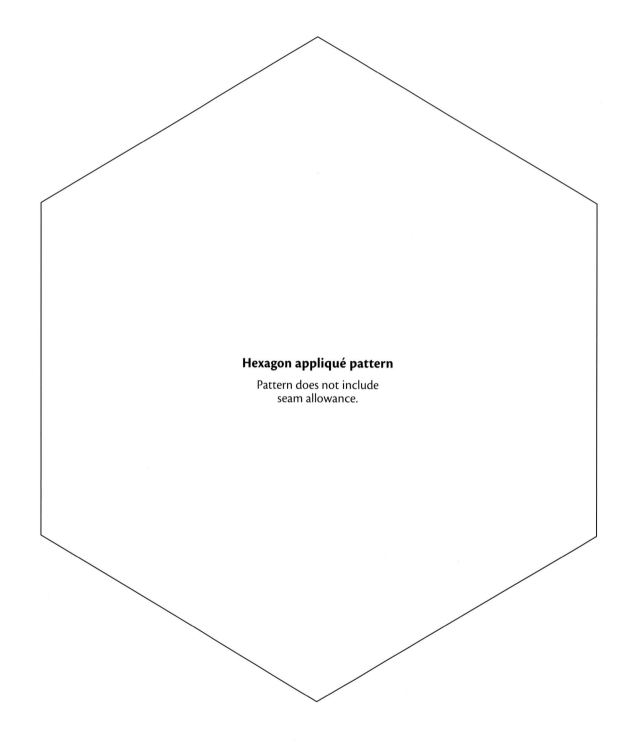

Hexagon appliqué pattern

Pattern does not include
seam allowance.

Umbrellas

The pillow and wall hanging together make a lively duet that is as fresh as a spring rain. Here's a good excuse to use happy fabrics for the pieced-and-appliquéd umbrellas.

FINISHED PILLOW: 16" X 16" • FINISHED QUILT: 32" X 44"

MATERIALS

Materials listed here are sufficient to make both the wall hanging and the pillow. Yardage is based on 42"-wide fabric and fat quarters are based on an 18" x 20" cut.

For the pillow and wall hanging

9 fat quarters of assorted prints for umbrella appliqués and pillow backing (use more for variety, if desired)

1½ yards of dark floral print for pillow background and piping and wall-hanging border, sashing, and binding

1⅓ yards of light floral print for wall-hanging background, sashing, border, binding, and one pillow umbrella appliqué

⅛ yard *total* of two different dark fabrics for handle appliqués

Freezer paper

For the pillow

¾ yard of lightweight muslin for backing and lining

21" x 21" square of batting

2 yards of ⁵⁄₃₂"-diameter cotton cording

3 assorted-size buttons, ⅝" and larger, to cover

16" pillow form

For the wall hanging

1⅔ yards of fabric for backing and sleeve

36" x 48" piece of batting

Cutting

All measurements include ¼"-wide seam allowances. Cut all pieces across the width of the fabric unless otherwise noted.

Refer to "Making Templates" (page 11) and use patterns A–C (page 40) to make templates for piecing the umbrellas. Plan your umbrella placement and fabric choices for the pillow and wall hanging before cutting out any of the fabric pieces. Cut sets of pieces from the same fabric.

For the pillow and wall hanging

From the assorted fat quarters, cut:
1 piece, 12" x 17", from *each* of 2 different fat quarters for pillow back
6 sets of 6 pieces using template A for pillow
15 sets of 6 pieces using template A for wall hanging
2 sets of 1 piece using template B, 1 piece using template C, and 1 piece using template C reversed for pillow
8 sets of 1 piece using template B, 1 piece using template C, and 1 piece using template C reversed for wall hanging

From the *lengthwise grain* of the light floral print, cut:
3 strips, 8½" x 40½", for wall hanging

From the remainder of the light floral print, cut:
6 squares, 2½" x 2½", for wall hanging
2 strips, 1¾" x 17", for wall hanging
1 set of 6 pieces using template A for pillow

From the dark floral print, cut:
3 strips, 1¾" x 42", for wall hanging
1 square, 18" x 18", for pillow background

From the *lengthwise grain* of the dark floral print, cut:
1 piece, 2½" x 37½", for wall hanging
1 piece, 2½" x 36½", for wall hanging
1 piece, 2½" x 23½", for wall hanging
1 piece, 2½" x 18½", for wall hanging
1 piece, 2½" x 15½", for wall hanging
1 piece, 2½" x 13½", for wall hanging
6 pieces, 2½" x 8½", for wall hanging
1 piece, 2½" x 7½", for wall hanging
1 piece, 2½" x 6½", for wall hanging
1 piece, 2½" x 5½", for wall hanging
1 piece, 2½" x 4½", for wall hanging

From the *bias* of the remaining dark floral print, cut:
Enough 1"-wide strips to make a 68"-long strip when joined end to end for pillow

For the pillow

From the muslin, cut:
1 square, 21" x 21"
2 rectangles, 7" x 17"

For the wall hanging

From the fabric for backing and sleeve, cut:
1 piece, 36" x 48"
Set aside the remaining fabric for making a sleeve, if desired.

Pillow

PREPARING AND APPLIQUÉING THE UMBRELLAS

1. Use a chalk pencil or other removable marking tool to draw lines 1" from all four sides on the right side of the dark floral 18" square.

2. To make the top-view umbrellas, using the matching A pieces from one set, sew two triangles together, matching the centers and ends. Finger-press the seam allowances open. Sew a third triangle to the pair and finger-press the seam allowances open. Repeat with the remaining three matching triangles to make two umbrella halves. Sew the halves together, paying careful attention to match the center intersection and seam lines. Press the seam allowances open. With an iron, firmly press the entire piece. Repeat to make a total of seven top-view umbrellas.

Note: If you're using a directional print, you may want to experiment with the arrangement of the triangles before sewing them together. Grain line isn't as important as the design, so it doesn't matter how you rotate the triangles.

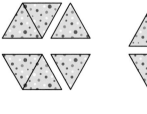

3. For the side-view umbrellas, using the matching B, C, and C reversed pieces from one set, clip the inner curved seam on the C and C reversed pieces almost to the seam line. Pin, and then sew the C piece to the B piece, matching the centers, ends, and along the seam line. Because this is a curve, it's helpful to use lots of pins. This step takes extra time, but pinning will make a nicer curve. Finger-press the seam allowances open. Repeat with the C reversed piece on the opposite side of the B piece. With an iron, firmly press the entire piece. Repeat to make a total of two side-view umbrellas.

Match seam lines.

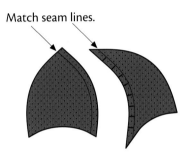

4. Referring to "Freezer-Paper Appliqué" (page 11) and using the top-view and side-view appliqué patterns (page 41), trace three top-view shapes and one side-view shape onto the non-shiny side of a piece of freezer paper and cut them out. Using the umbrella handle appliqué pattern (page 40), trace two umbrella handles onto freezer paper and cut them out. You'll reuse some of the templates.

5. Refer to "Freezer-Paper Appliqué" and use the freezer-paper templates to prepare two umbrella handles from the dark handle fabric.

6. Center the top-view freezer-paper templates, shiny side down, onto the wrong side of three top-view umbrella pieces, matching the points of the templates with the seam lines. Trim the seam allowance if necessary to slightly less than ¼". Clip curves almost to the template. Finger-press the seam allowance over the template.

Repeat the process with the side-view freezer-paper template and a side-view umbrella piece.

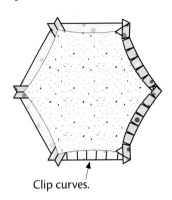

Clip curves.

7. Referring to the photo (page 36) as a guide, arrange the prepared umbrellas within the marked lines of the pillow top as desired, positioning the straight end of a prepared handle appliqué about ⅜" under the center bottom edge of the side-view umbrella. When you're happy with the placement, pin the pieces in place. Appliqué the pieces in place, removing the freezer-paper templates using method 2 for the umbrellas and method 1 for the handles.

8. Repeat steps 6 and 7 with the remaining umbrellas.

FINISHING THE PILLOW

Follow the instructions under "Pillow Construction" (page 14) to finish constructing the pillow. Use the raindrop quilting pattern (page 40), if desired, to quilt the pillow top.

Wall Hanging

PREPARING THE APPLIQUÉS

Refer to steps 2–6 of "Preparing and Appliquéing the Umbrellas" (page 36) to prepare 15 top-view umbrella appliqués, eight side-view umbrella appliqués, four umbrella handle appliqués, and four reversed umbrella handle appliqués. You will need five top-view umbrella freezer-paper templates, three side-view umbrella freezer-paper templates, two handle freezer-paper templates, and two reversed handle freezer-paper templates. You'll reuse the templates.

ASSEMBLING THE WALL-HANGING TOP

1. Sew dark floral print 2½" x 8½" pieces to the short ends of each light floral 8½" x 40½" strip. Press the seam allowances toward the dark floral pieces.

Make 3.

2. Assemble the remaining dark floral and light floral 2½" squares as shown to make the vertical sashing strips. Press the seam allowances toward the dark floral pieces.

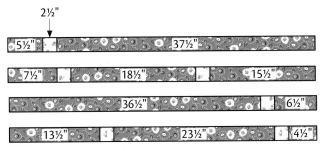

Make 1 of each.

3. Sew the pieces from steps 1 and 2 together. Press the seam allowances toward the sashing strips.

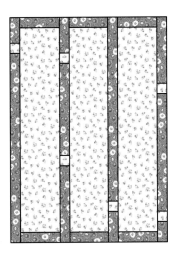

4. Referring to the photo (page 38) as a guide, arrange the prepared umbrella appliqués on one panel of the wall-hanging top as desired, positioning the straight end of a prepared handle appliqué about ⅜" under the center bottom edge of the side-view umbrella. When you're happy with the placement, pin the pieces in place. Appliqué the pieces in place, removing the freezer-paper templates using method 2 for the umbrella and method 1 for the handle. Repeat with the remaining umbrellas.

FINISHING THE WALL HANGING

Refer to "Wall-Hanging Construction" (page 17) as needed.

1. Layer the wall-hanging top with batting and backing; baste the layers together.
2. Quilt, referring to the photos (on the previous pages) for ideas and using the raindrop quilting pattern (page 40), if desired.
3. Bind opposite corners of the wall hanging using the light floral 1¾" x 17" strips. Place the center of each strip at the corner to begin, and then work back toward one end, pinning as you go. When sewing the binding strips in place, leave about 4" unsewn at both ends so you can join the strips to the dark floral 1¾" strips. When both corners have been bound, add the dark floral binding strip to the remainder of the edges, joining it to the light floral strips.
4. Add a hanging sleeve and label, if desired.

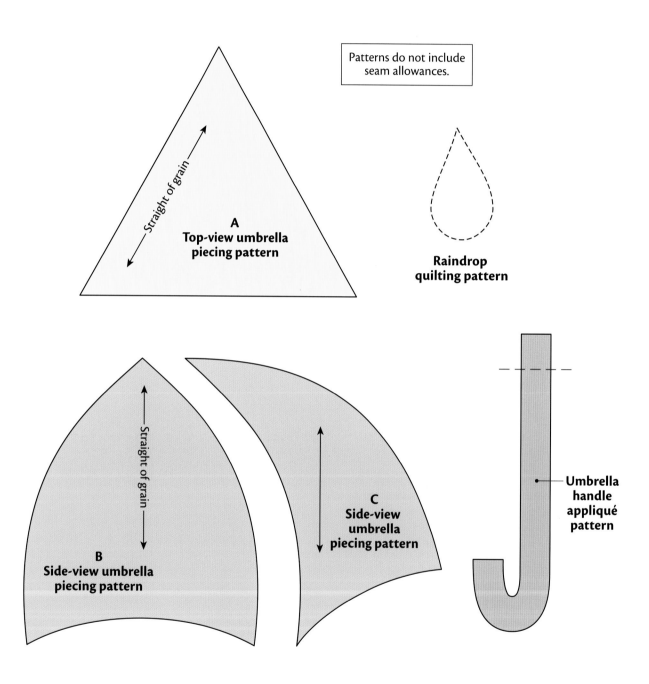

Patterns do not include
seam allowances.

A
Top-view umbrella
piecing pattern

Straight of grain

Raindrop
quilting pattern

B
Side-view umbrella
piecing pattern

Straight of grain

C
Side-view
umbrella
piecing pattern

Umbrella
handle
appliqué
pattern

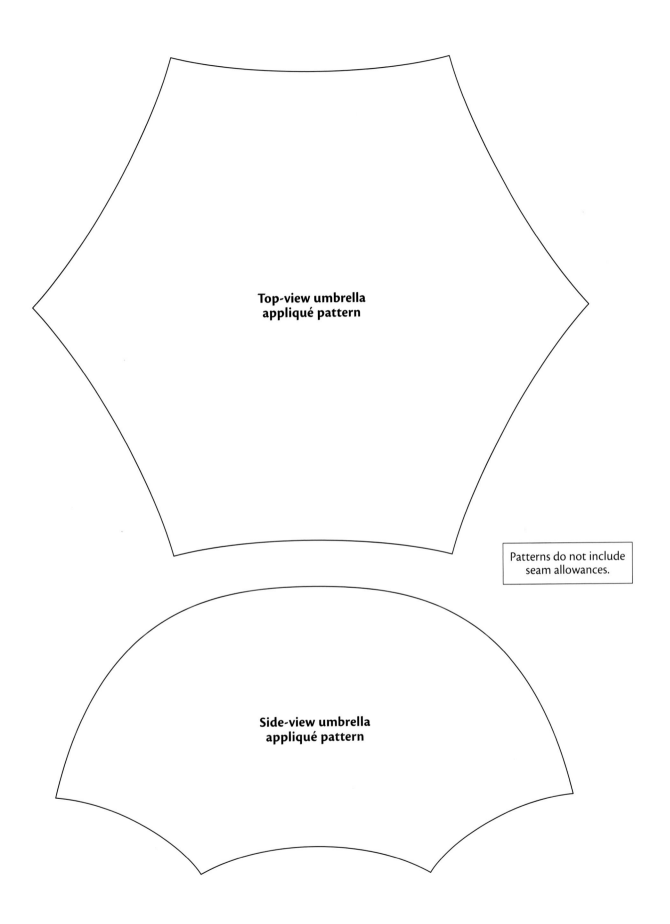

**Top-view umbrella
appliqué pattern**

Patterns do not include
seam allowances.

**Side-view umbrella
appliqué pattern**

Spring Baskets

This cheerful pillow and wall-hanging set uses sunny spring fabrics to brighten any room. Old-fashioned string piecing is updated with an easy piecing method to stitch these geometric baskets.

FINISHED PILLOW: 16" x 16" • FINISHED PILLOW BLOCK: 7" x 7"
FINISHED QUILT: 36" x 46" • FINISHED QUILT BLOCK: 10" x 10"

MATERIALS

Materials listed here are sufficient to make both the wall hanging and the pillow. Yardage is based on 42"-wide fabric and fat quarters are based on an 18" x 20" cut.

The baskets in this project are made using string piecing, an old piecing method that uses various widths of scraps. Even the very narrowest strips can be frugally used. While the following materials list specifies newly purchased fabrics for the string quilting, you can also use scraps.

For the pillow and wall hanging

8 assorted fat quarters or scraps for basket strings
1⅝ yards of floral print for borders and wall-hanging binding
1⅛ yards of light solid for backgrounds
2¼ yards of fabric for pillow back, wall-hanging backing, and wall-hanging sleeve
Foundation paper

For the pillow

1 fat quarter *each* of 2 assorted dark fabrics for basket bases, handles, and strings
¾ yard of lightweight muslin for backing and lining
¼ yard of dark blue fabric for piping
21" x 21" square of batting
2 yards of ⁵⁄₃₂"-diameter cotton cording
3 assorted-size buttons, ⅝" and larger, to cover
16" pillow form

For the wall hanging

1½ yards of dark fabric for basket bases, handles, and wall-hanging border
40" x 50" piece of batting

CUTTING

All measurements include ¼"-wide seam allowances. Cut all pieces across the width of the fabric unless otherwise noted. Refer to "Cutting Strings" (below) before cutting strips for piecing the baskets. Refer to "Making Templates" (page 11) and use patterns A and B (page 50) to make templates for the block side pieces.

Cutting Strings

Whenever the word "string" is used it refers to a strip of fabric, cut an uneven width. To cut the strings, lay a rotary cutter along the lengthwise grain of the fabric at a slight angle so that it isn't parallel to the edge. Strips should be 1" to 2" wide and vary in width from one end to the other. Cut the string. Extra strings are cut for more variety when piecing.

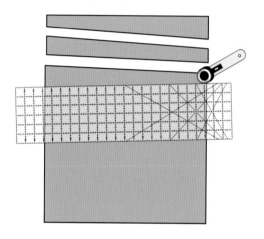

For the pillow and wall hanging

From the *lengthwise grain* of *each* of the 8 fat quarters, cut:
2 strings in various widths from 1" to 2" x 18" for pillow (16 total)
6 strings in various widths from 1" to 2" x 18" for wall hanging (48 total)

From the light solid fabric, cut:
2 squares, 6" x 6"; cut in half diagonally to make 4 triangles for pillow
6 squares, 8¼" x 8¼"; cut in half diagonally to make 12 triangles for wall hanging
4 and 4 reversed using template A for pillow
12 and 12 reversed using template B for wall hanging

From the *lengthwise grain* of the floral print, cut:
4 strips, 1¾" x 48", for wall hanging
4 strips, 1¾" x 38", for wall hanging
4 strips, 2" x 17", for pillow
2 strings in various widths from 1" to 2" x 18" for pillow
4 strings in various widths from 1" to 2" x 18" for wall hanging

From the remainder of the floral print, cut:
Enough 1¾"-wide strips to make a 174"-long strip when joined end to end for wall hanging

From the fabric for pillow back and wall-hanging backing, cut:
2 pieces, 12" x 17", for pillow
1 piece, 40" x 50", for wall hanging
Set aside the remaining fabric for making a wall-hanging sleeve, if desired.

For the pillow

From *each* of the 2 assorted fat quarters of dark fabric, cut:
1 square, 3½" x 3½"; cut in half diagonally to make 2 triangles (4 total)
2 strings in various widths from 1" to 2" x 18"

From the bias of the remaining fat quarters of dark fabric, cut:
4 strips, 1" x 10"

From the muslin, cut:
1 square, 21" x 21"
2 pieces, 7" x 17"

From the *bias* of the dark blue fabric, cut:
Enough 1"-wide strips to make a 68"-long strip when joined end to end for pillow

For the wall hanging

From the *lengthwise grain* of the dark fabric, cut:
2 strips, 1" x 38"
2 strips, 1" x 48"
6 squares, 4" x 4"; cut in half diagonally to make 12 triangles

From the *bias* of the remaining dark fabric, cut:
12 strips, 1" x 12", for wall hanging

Pillow

MAKING THE BASKET BLOCKS

1. Using the pillow foundation pattern (page 49), trace four foundations onto foundation paper. Cut out each one slightly beyond the outer lines.

2. To string piece each foundation, turn over the foundation to the unmarked side. Starting at the top of the trapezoid, lay a fabric string right side up across the foundation so it covers the outer cutting lines. Lay the next string over the first string, right sides together, making sure the bottom edge of the second strip is on the first strip and that the entire width of the foundation is covered. It can be parallel with the first strip or placed at a slight angle. Stitch ¼" from the bottom edge of the second string. Trim the seam allowances to ¼" if necessary, and then press piece 2 to the right side with a dry iron. Continue adding more strings until the entire foundation is covered.

3. Press the completed foundations from the fabric side with a dry iron. Turn over each foundation to the paper side and trim on the outer cutting lines. Leave the paper on until the block is completed.

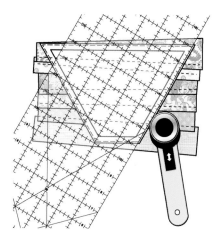

4. On the right side of each of the four light triangles, mark the handle placement using the guide (page 51). Refer to "Bias-Strip Appliqué" (page 13) to prepare the four dark fabric 1" x 10" bias strips for appliqué. Pin a prepared bias strip to each triangle following the placement lines and using lots of pins. Appliqué the outer curves first, removing pins as you go. On inner curves, pin as you gather the excess fabric evenly. Appliqué in place. Trim the excess handle fabric even with the edge of the triangles.

5. Sew a handle triangle from step 4 to the top edge of each string-pieced unit. Then sew the A and A reversed pieces to the sides of the string-pieced unit. Add a dark fabric triangle to the bottom of each of these units. Press all the seam allowances away from the string-pieced unit. Remove all of the foundation paper from each block. Trim the blocks to 7½" square.

ASSEMBLING THE PILLOW TOP

1. Arrange the blocks into two rows of two blocks each, with the bases meeting in the center and alternating the fabrics. Sew the blocks in each row together. Press the seam allowances open. Sew the rows together. Press the seam allowances open.

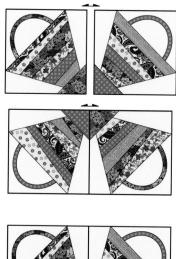

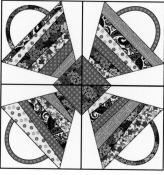

2. Refer to "Adding Borders" (page 17) to sew the floral print 2" x 17" border strips to the pillow top; miter the corners.

FINISHING THE PILLOW

Follow the instructions under "Pillow Construction" (page 14) to finish constructing the pillow.

Wall Hanging

ASSEMBLING THE WALL-HANGING TOP

1. Refer to steps 1–5 of "Making the Basket Blocks" (page 45) for the pillow to make 12 blocks using the wall-hanging foundation pattern (page 50), the wall-hanging basket handle placement guide (page 51), the dark 1" x 12" bias strips, and the template B pieces. Trim the blocks to 10½" square.

2. Arrange the blocks into four rows of three blocks each, with all of the block handles in the upper-left corner. Sew the blocks in each row together. Press the seam allowances open. Sew the rows together, matching the block intersections and the points where the baskets meet. Press the seam allowances open.

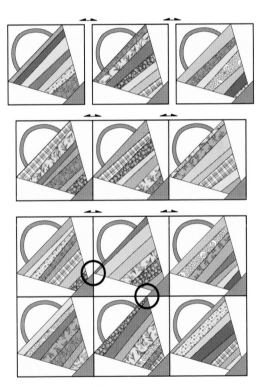

Match points.

3. Sew floral 1¾" x 38" strips to both long edges of a dark fabric 1" x 38" strip. Press the seam allowances toward the dark strip. Repeat to make a total of two border strips for the wall-hanging top and bottom. Repeat with the floral and dark 48"-long strips to make the side borders.

Top/bottom border.
Make 2.

Side border.
Make 2.

4. Refering to "Adding Borders" (page 17), attach the borders and miter the corners.

FINISHING THE WALL HANGING

Refer to "Wall-Hanging Construction" (page 17).

1. Layer the wall-hanging top with batting and backing; baste the layers together.
2. Quilt, referring to the photos (on the previous pages) for ideas. For an original quilt design, try copying and enlarging a floral design from one of the fabrics.
3. The border for this wall hanging was cut slightly oversized; after quilting, trim it to about 3" wide to square up the quilt.
4. Bind the wall hanging with the floral print 1¾"-wide strips.
5. Add a hanging sleeve and label, if desired.

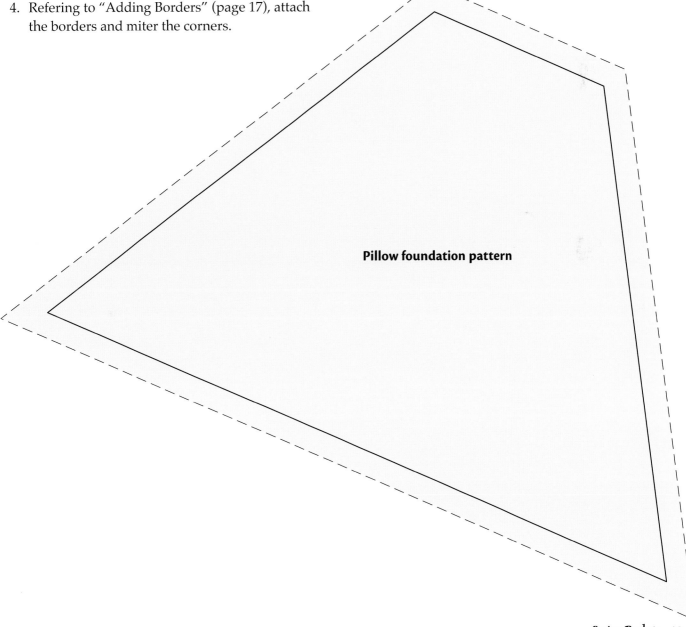

Pillow foundation pattern

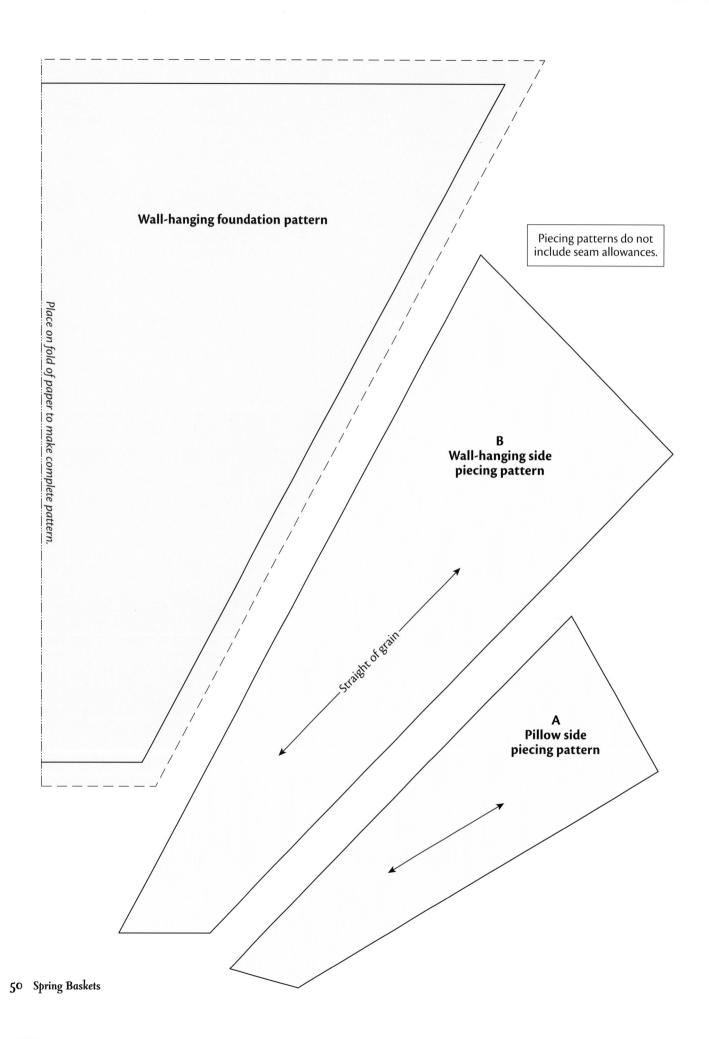

Wall-hanging foundation pattern

Place on fold of paper to make complete pattern.

Piecing patterns do not include seam allowances.

B
Wall-hanging side piecing pattern

Straight of grain

A
Pillow side piecing pattern

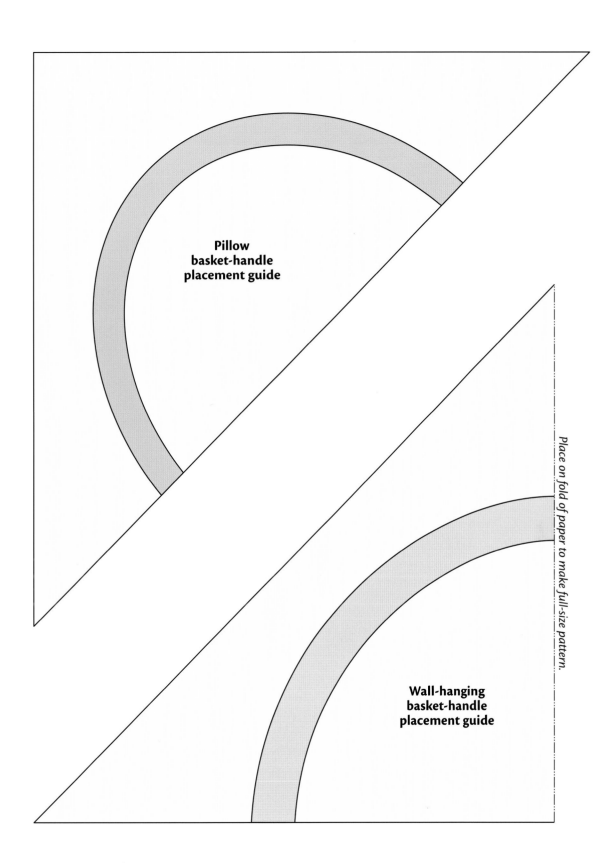

**Pillow
basket-handle
placement guide**

**Wall-hanging
basket-handle
placement guide**

Place on fold of paper to make full-size pattern.

Summer Flowers

This pillow and wall-hanging duo are perfect for injecting a cool summer mood into your decor anytime! Three easy blocks combine with a touch of appliqué and embroidery for two quick, simple projects.

FINISHED PILLOW: 16" x 16" • FINISHED QUILT: 33" x 18"

FINISHED BLOCKS: 3" x 3"

MATERIALS

Materials listed here are sufficient to make both the pillow and the wall hanging. Yardage is based on 42"-wide fabric and fat quarters are based on an 18" x 20" cut.

For the pillow and wall hanging

1⅛ yards of dark blue fabric for flowers, borders, pillow piping, and wall-hanging binding (use an assortment for variety, if desired)

⅝ yard of white-on-white print for backgrounds

⅝ yard of green solid for leaves and stems

6 fat quarters *total* of assorted green and blue prints for blocks (use an assortment for variety, if desired)

1⅜ yards of fabric for pillow back, wall-hanging backing, and wall-hanging sleeve

Freezer paper

Blue and green embroidery floss

Size 9 embroidery needle

For the pillow

¾ yard of lightweight muslin for backing and lining

21" x 21" square of batting

2 yards of ⁵⁄₃₂"-diameter cotton cording

3 assorted-size buttons, ⅝" and larger, to cover

16" pillow form

For the wall hanging

22" x 37" piece of batting

Cutting

*All measurements include ¼"-wide seam allowances.
Cut all pieces across the width of the fabric unless otherwise noted.*

For the pillow and wall hanging

**From the *lengthwise grain* of the white-on-white
print, cut:**
4 strips, 1¾" x 18", for pillow
6 strips, 1¾" x 18", for wall hanging

**From the remainder of the white-on-white
print, cut:**
12 squares, 2½" x 2½", for pillow
24 squares, 2½" x 2½", for wall hanging

**From the *lengthwise grain* of the dark blue
fabric, cut:**
2 strips, 2" x 34", for wall hanging
2 strips, 2" x 19", for wall hanging
4 strips, 1½" x 18", for pillow

From the remainder of the dark blue fabric, cut:
Enough 1¾"-wide strips to make a 112"-long strip
    when joined end to end for wall hanging
12 squares, 2½" x 2½", for pillow
24 squares, 2½" x 2½", for wall hanging

**From the *bias* of the remaining dark blue
fabric, cut:**
Enough 1"-wide strips to make a 68"-long strip
    when joined end to end for pillow

From the *lengthwise grain* of the green solid, cut:
2 strips, 1" x 18", for pillow
3 strips, 1" x 18", for wall hanging

From the *bias* of the remaining green solid, cut:
2 strips, 1" x 8", for pillow
1 strip, 1" x 11", for pillow
4 strips, 1" x 8", for wall hanging
1 strip, 1" x 11", for wall hanging

**From the *lengthwise grain* of the green and blue
prints, cut a *total* of:**
16 strips, 1¼" x 18", for pillow
28 strips, 1¼" x 18", for wall hanging

**From the fabric for pillow back and wall-hanging
backing, cut:**
2 pieces, 12" x 17", for pillow
1 piece, 37" x 22", for wall hanging
Set aside the remaining fabric for making a
    wall-hanging sleeve, if desired.

For the pillow

From the muslin, cut:
1 square, 21" x 21"
2 pieces, 7" x 17"

Pillow

MAKING THE BLOCKS

1. To make the Pinwheel Flower blocks, draw a diagonal line from corner to corner on the wrong side of each white 2½" square. Lay a marked square right sides together with a dark blue 2½" square. Sew ¼" from both sides of the marked line. Cut the squares apart on the marked line to yield two half-square-triangle units. Press the seam allowances toward the blue triangle. Trim each unit to 2" square. Repeat to make a total of 24 units.

Make 24.

2. Arrange four half-square-triangle units into two rows of two units each to make a pinwheel shape. Sew the units in each row together. Press the seam allowances open. Sew the rows together. Press the seam allowances open. Repeat to make a total of six blocks.

Pinwheel Flower block.
Make 6.

3. To make the Stem blocks, sew white 1¾" x 18" strips to both long edges of a green 1" x 18" strip to make a strip set. Repeat to make a total of two strip sets. Press the seam allowances toward the green strips. Crosscut the strip sets into six segments, 3½" wide, to make the blocks.

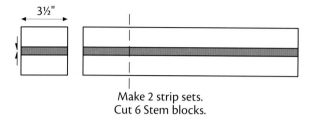

Make 2 strip sets.
Cut 6 Stem blocks.

4. To make the Strip blocks, join four different green and blue 1¼" x 18" strips along the long edges to make a strip set. Press the seam allowances open. Repeat to make a total of four different strip sets. Crosscut the strips sets into 16 segments, 3½" wide, to make the blocks.

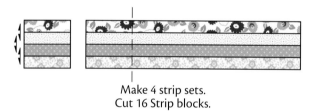

Make 4 strip sets.
Cut 16 Strip blocks.

ASSEMBLING THE PILLOW TOP

1. Lay out the Pinwheel Flower blocks, Stem blocks, and 13 of the Strip blocks into five vertical rows of five blocks each. You have three extra Strip blocks to work with so you can play with variety in the arrangement. Sew the blocks in each row together. Press the seam allowances open between the Pinwheel Flower and Stem blocks and between two Strip blocks; press all of the remaining seam allowances toward the Strip blocks. Sew the rows together. Press the seam allowances open.

2. Refer to "Bias-Strip Appliqué" (page 13) to prepare the green 1" x 8" and 1" x 11" bias strips for appliqué. Refer to "Freezer-Paper Appliqué" (page 11) and use the leaf-circle appliqué pattern (page 57) to trace four leaf circles onto the dull side of a piece of freezer paper and cut them out. Use the freezer-paper templates to prepare four leaf circles from the remaining green fabric. You will reuse the templates.

3. Referring to the photo (page 55), position the bias stems on the quilt top, curving them as desired. When you're happy with the placement, pin the pieces in place. At the point where the bias stems meet the Stem blocks, you may want to rip out a few stitches of the seam, tuck in the end of the bias strip, and then re-sew the seam to make a smoother transition. If not, turn the ends under. Appliqué the edges of the stems in place. Position the leaf appliqués next to and on the stems as desired, and then

appliqué them in place, removing the freezer-paper templates using the desired method. Use the removed templates two more times to prepare seven additional leaves and appliqué them in place.

4. Refer to "Adding Borders" (page 17) to sew the dark blue 1½" x 18" border strips to the pillow top; miter the corners.

5. Referring to the pattern at right and using two strands of blue embroidery floss and a stem stitch, freehand stitch a curved line on the white triangle of each flower. Stitch a French knot at the end of each line. With two strands of green embroidery floss, backstitch the detail lines on each leaf using the pattern at right as a reference.

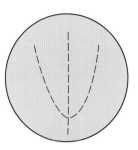

Leaf-circle appliqué and embroidery pattern

Appliqué pattern does not include seam allowance.

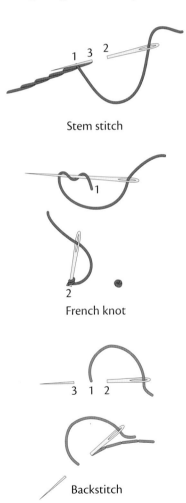

Stem stitch

French knot

Backstitch

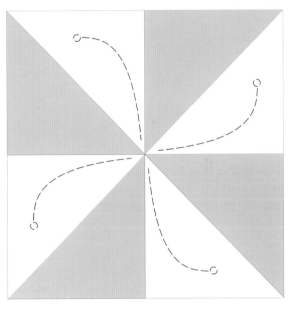

Pinwheel Flower embroidery pattern

FINISHING THE PILLOW

Follow the instructions under "Pillow Construction" (page 14) to finish constructing the pillow.

Wall Hanging

ASSEMBLING THE
WALL-HANGING TOP

1. Refer to steps 1–4 of "Making the Blocks" (page 55) for the pillow to make the blocks with the following changes. For the Pinwheel Flower blocks, make 12. For the Stem blocks, make three strip sets and cut 12 blocks. For the Strip blocks, make seven strip sets and cut 28 blocks (you will have two extra).

2. Lay out the Pinwheel Flower blocks, the Stem blocks, and 26 of the Strip blocks into 10 vertical rows of five blocks each. You have two extra Strip blocks to work with, so you can play with variety in the arrangement. Sew the blocks in each row together. Press the seam allowances open between the Pinwheel and Stem blocks

and between two Strip blocks; press all of the remaining seam allowances toward the Strip blocks. Sew the rows together. Press the seam allowances open.

3. Refer to steps 2–5 of "Assembling the Pillow Top" (page 56) to finish constructing the wall-hanging top, making six leaf freezer-paper templates to create 18 leaf appliques and using the dark blue 2" x 19" strips for the side borders and the 2" x 34" strips for the top and bottom borders.

FINISHING THE WALL HANGING

Refer to "Wall-Hanging Construction" (page 17).
1. Layer the wall-hanging top with batting and backing; baste the layers together.
2. Quilt as desired, referring to the photos (on the previous pages) for ideas.
3. The border for this quilt was cut slightly oversized; after quilting, trim it to about 1½" to square up the quilt.
4. Bind the quilt using the dark blue 1¾"-wide strips.
5. Add a hanging sleeve and label, if desired.

Hot!

Add a lively, bold accent to your summer decorating with this colorful pillow-and-wall-hanging combo. Raw-edge machine appliqué is quick and easy and makes this project fun to stitch.

FINISHED PILLOW: 16" X 16" • FINISHED WALL HANGING: 37" X 37"

MATERIALS

Materials listed here are sufficient to make both the wall hanging and the pillow. Yardage is based on 42"-wide fabric and fat quarters are based on an 18" x 20" cut.

For the pillow and wall hanging

2⅛ yards of bright medium blue print for backgrounds, pillow piping, and wall-hanging binding
⅝ yard of bright yellow solid fabric for sashing
7 fat quarters and/or scraps of assorted bright prints to coordinate with background fabric for appliqués and pillow back
Spray starch
Template plastic
Tear-away stabilizer

For the pillow

¾ yard of lightweight muslin for backing and lining
21" x 21" square of batting
2 yards of ⁵⁄₃₂"-diameter cotton cording
3 assorted-size buttons, ⅝" and larger, to cover
16" pillow form

For the wall hanging

1½ yards of fabric for backing and sleeve
41" x 41" square of batting

CUTTING

All measurements include ¼"-wide seam allowances. Cut all pieces across the width of the fabric unless otherwise noted.

For the pillow and wall hanging

From the bright medium blue print, cut:
4 strips, 1¾" x 42", for wall hanging
1 square, 38" x 38", for wall hanging
1 square, 18" x 18", for pillow

From the *bias* of the remaining bright medium blue fabric, cut:
Enough 1"-wide strips to make a 68"-long strip when joined end to end for pillow

From the *lengthwise grain* of *each* of 2 fat quarters, cut:
1 piece, 12" x 17", for pillow

For the pillow

From the muslin, cut:
1 square, 21" x 21"
2 pieces, 7" x 17"

For the wall hanging

From the fabric for backing and sleeve, cut:
1 piece, 41" x 41"
Set aside the remaining fabric for making a hanging sleeve, if desired.

Pillow

Preparing and Cutting the Appliqué Pieces

1. Liberally apply spray starch to the yellow solid sashing fabric and each of the fat quarters and/or scraps of fabric for appliqués (do not starch the 12" x 17" pieces you cut from the two fat quarters, but do starch any of the remaining fabric).

2. Trace patterns A–G onto template plastic and cut them out on the drawn lines.

3. To make the sashing appliqués, place template A onto the wrong side of the yellow solid fabric and trace around it with a pencil or a marking tool. Do not use pen because it may bleed through. To keep the fabric from slipping, lay it on a board covered with fine-grit sandpaper. Rotate the template so the curve is angled in the opposite direction and align the end of the

template with the end of the marked shape. Repeat to make a total of four sashing strips. Cut out the strips.

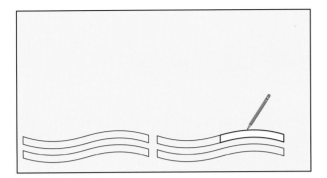

4. To make the triangle and circle appliqués, trace a total of 32 shapes using templates B–F and a total of 11 shapes using template G onto the wrong side of the fat quarters and/or scraps and trace around them. Cut out each shape. Also cut six strips, ⅜" x 6".

Assembling the Pillow Top

1. On the right side of the bright medium blue 18" square, lay a ruler 2" from one edge. Place a sashing strip next to the ruler so the end of the strip and the convex curved edge touch it. Pin, hand baste, or use spray adhesive to baste the strip in place.

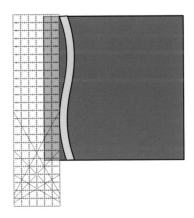

2. Place a piece of stabilizer on the wrong side of the square beneath the sashing strip. Thread your sewing machine and wind the bobbin with a cotton or cotton-blend thread that coordinates or contrasts with the sashing strip. You can use polyester thread but be careful when ironing because the heat may melt the thread.

Set your sewing machine for a narrow zigzag stitch, blanket stitch, or decorative stitch of your choice. Experiment on a sample piece before stitching the pillow top to determine which one you like best. Beginning in the middle of the strip, stitch along both long edges of the sashing strip. Tear away the stabilizer. Repeat on the opposite edge of the pillow to add the next strip, and then add the remaining strips to the remaining two edges, removing the stabilizer after each strip is stitched in place.

Stabilizer Substitutes

If you don't have any stabilizer on hand, look around the house for a suitable substitute. You will need a lightweight paper that tears away easily. Gift-wrap tissue paper is a good choice. Just be sure to iron out any wrinkles. Calligraphy paper also works well.

3. Arrange the triangles, circles, and strips on the pillow top, referring to the photo for approximate placements. Extra pieces were cut to allow for arrangement choices so you do not have to use them all. When you're satisfied with the arrangement, pin or baste the pieces in place. Machine appliqué the shapes in place using stabilizer underneath and working on one "burst" at a time. After the pieces in each area are sewn, carefully pull the loose threads to the back and knot them together; trim the ends. Remove the stabilizer.

Finishing the Pillow

Follow the instructions under "Pillow Construction" (page 14) to finish constructing the pillow.

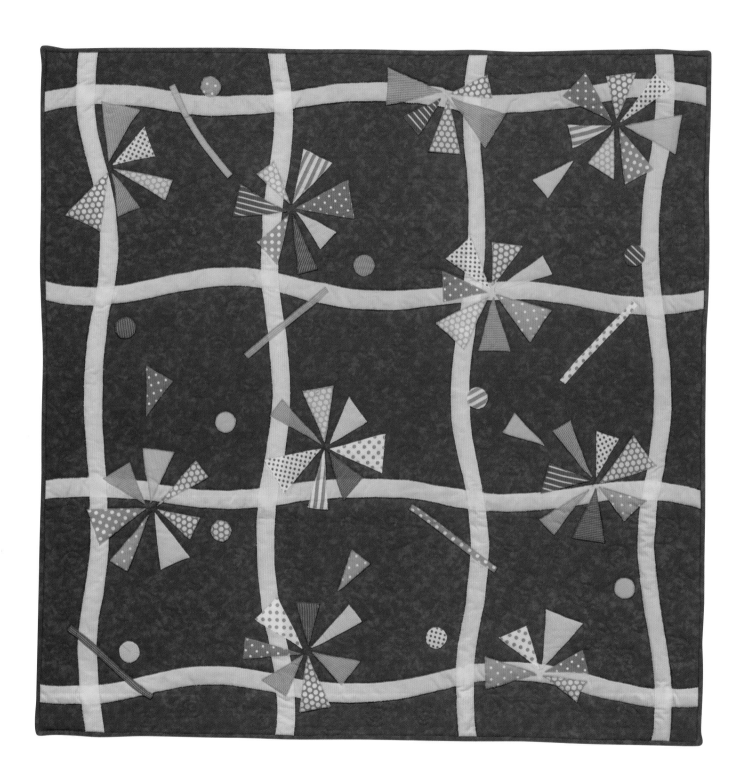

Wall Hanging

ASSEMBLING THE WALL-HANGING TOP

1. Refer to steps 1 and 2 of "Preparing and Cutting the Appliqué Pieces" (page 62) for the pillow to prepare the fabrics and make the templates. Refer to step 3 to trace as many template A shapes as possible (about 4½) end to end onto the wrong side of the remaining yellow solid fabric to make a sashing strip. Repeat to make a total of eight strips.

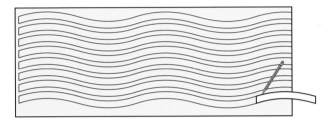

2. From the remaining fat quarters cut seven strips, ⅜" x 6", and make a total of 74 shapes using templates B–F and 12 using template G.

3. Mark the center of the bright medium blue 38" square. Lay a ruler on the square so that a straight line is formed 4½" to the right of the center mark and parallel to the outer edge. Lay a sashing strip along the edge of the ruler with the convex curved edges just touching the ruler. Pin or baste the strip in place. Referring to step 2 of "Assembling the Pillow Top" (page 63), machine appliqué along the long edges of the strip, beginning in the middle. Remove the stabilizer and trim the excess sashing even with the edges of the square.

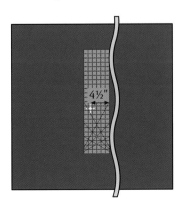

4. Lay a second sashing strip parallel to the first and 4½" to the left of the center mark, again using a ruler to keep the strip "straight." If desired, reverse the direction of the curves so they are opposite from the first strip. Appliqué the strip in place in the same manner as the first; trim and remove the stabilizer. Add one additional strip 9" to 10" to the right of the first strip and one additional strip 9" to 10" to the left of the second strip; trim and remove the stabilizer.

5. Rotate the background square 90° and repeat the process with the remaining four sashing strips.

6. Arrange the triangles, circles, and strips on the wall-hanging top, referring to the photo for approximate placements. Extra pieces were cut to allow for arrangement choices. Appliqué the shapes in place, using stabilizer on the wrong side of the background square. Remove all of the stabilizer after stitching and secure the threads.

FINISHING THE WALL HANGING

Refer to "Wall-Hanging Construction" (page 17).
1. Layer the wall-hanging top with batting and backing; baste the layers together.
2. Quilt as desired, referring to the photos (on the previous pages) for ideas and using the swirl quilting pattern (page 66), if desired.
3. Trim the wall hanging to 37" square.
4. Bind the wall hanging with the bright medium blue 1¾"-wide strips.
5. Add a hanging sleeve and label, if desired.

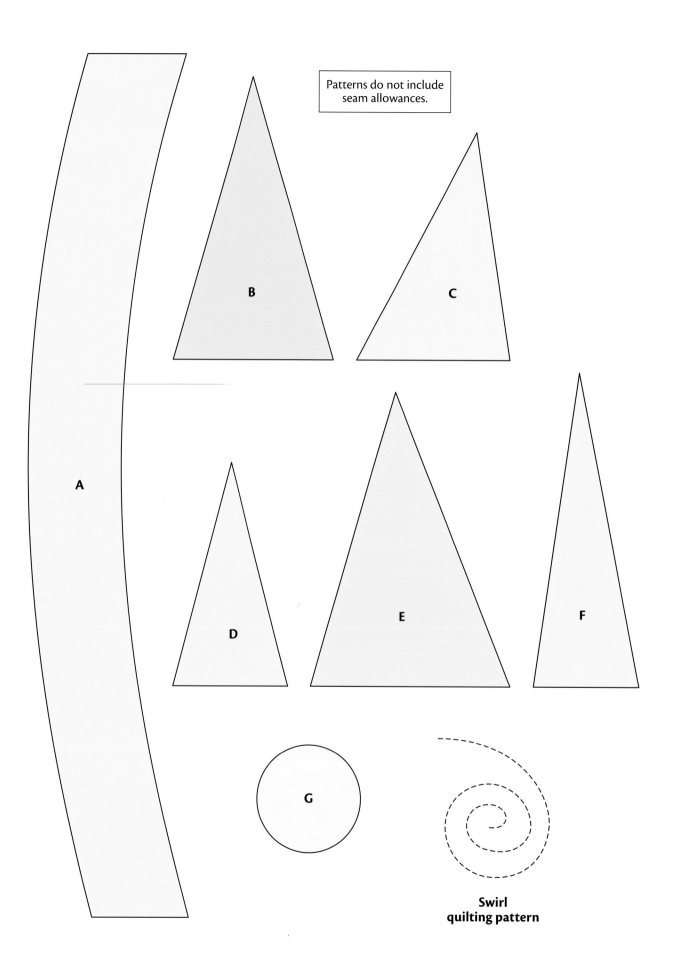

Patterns do not include seam allowances.

A

B

C

D

E

F

G

Swirl
quilting pattern

Fall Walk in the Park

The warm colors of this cozy pair remind me of a relaxed walk in a park in the fall. The strip-pieced background joins with easy freezer-paper appliqué to create a bird's-eye view of the scene. Add more gray, rust, and brown fabrics for even more variety.

FINISHED PILLOW: 16" x 16" • FINISHED QUILT: 40" x 49"

MATERIALS

Materials listed here are sufficient to make both the wall hanging and the pillow. Yardage is based on 42"-wide fabric and fat quarters are based on an 18" x 20" cut.

For the pillow and wall hanging

Label each gray fabric with the designated letter for cutting later.

3¼ yards of gray fabric (F) for backgrounds, pillow back, pillow piping, wall-hanging backing, and wall-hanging binding

½ yard *each* of 4 assorted gray fabrics (A, B, D, and E) for backgrounds and wall-hanging border

1⅜ yards of rust fabric for leaf appliqués, wall-hanging border, and wall-hanging sleeve

¾ yard of gray fabric (C) for backgrounds and wall-hanging border

3 fat quarters or scraps of assorted rust fabrics for leaf appliqués

3 fat quarters or scraps of assorted brown fabrics for branch appliqués

For the pillow

¾ yard of lightweight muslin for backing and lining
21" x 21" square of batting
2 yards of ⁵⁄₃₂"-diameter cotton cording
3 assorted-size square buttons, ⅝" and larger, to cover
16" pillow form

For the wall hanging

44" x 53" piece of batting

67

CUTTING

All measurements include a ¼"-wide seam allowances.
Cut all pieces across the width of the fabric unless other-
wise noted.

From gray fabric A, cut:
1 strip, 4½" x 11", for pillow
1 strip, 6½" x 15", for wall hanging
2 strips, 6½" x 12", for wall hanging
2 strips, 3½" x 15", for wall hanging
2 strips, 3½" x 7½", for wall hanging
1 square, 3½" x 3½", for wall hanging
1 rectangle, 3½" x 4", for wall hanging

From gray fabric B, cut:
1 strip, 4½" x 11", for pillow
1 strip, 2½" x 11", for pillow
1 strip, 6½" x 15", for wall hanging
2 strips, 6½" x 12", for wall hanging
3 strips, 3½" x 15", for wall hanging
1 square, 3½" x 3½", for wall hanging
1 rectangle, 3½" x 4", for wall hanging

From gray fabric C, cut:
2 strips, 4½" x 11", for pillow
2 strips, 6½" x 15", for wall hanging
2 strips, 6½" x 12", for wall hanging
2 strips, 3½" x 7½", for wall hanging
1 strip, 3½" x 15", for wall hanging
1 square, 3½" x 3½", for wall hanging
1 rectangle, 3½" x 4", for wall hanging

From gray fabric D, cut:
2 strips, 4½" x 11", for pillow
2 strips, 6½" x 15", for wall hanging
1 strip, 6½" x 12", for wall hanging
1 strip, 3½" x 15", for wall hanging
1 strip, 3½" x 12", for wall hanging
1 strip, 3½" x 7½", for wall hanging
2 rectangles, 3½" x 4", for wall hanging

From gray fabric E, cut:
1 strip, 4½" x 11", for pillow
1 strip, 2½" x 11", for pillow
2 strips, 6½" x 15", for wall hanging
1 strip, 6½" x 12", for wall hanging
1 strip, 3½" x 15", for wall hanging
1 strip, 3½" x 12", for wall hanging
1 strip, 3½" x 7½", for wall hanging
2 rectangles, 3½" x 4", for wall hanging

From the *lengthwise grain* of gray fabric F, cut:
1 piece, 42" x 53", for wall hanging
1 piece, 6" x 53", for wall hanging

From the remainder of gray fabric F, cut:
2 pieces, 12" x 17", for pillow
Enough 1¾"-wide strips to make a 188"-long strip
    when joined end to end for wall hanging
2 strips, 6½" x 15", for wall hanging
2 strips, 6½" x 12", for wall hanging
3 strips, 3½" x 7½", for wall hanging
1 square, 3½" x 3½", for wall hanging
1 rectangle, 3½" x 4", for wall hanging

From the *bias* of the remaining gray fabric F, cut:
Enough 1"-wide strips to make a 68"-long strip
    when joined end to end for pillow

For the pillow
From the muslin, cut:
1 square, 21" x 21"
2 pieces, 7" x 17"

For the wall hanging
From the *lengthwise grain* of the rust fabric, cut:
2 strips, 1" x 44"
2 strips, 1" x 35"
Set aside the remainder of the fabric for the leaf
    appliqués and a hanging sleeve, if desired.

Pillow

ASSEMBLING THE PILLOW TOP

1. Sew one 4½" x 11" strip *each* of gray fabrics B, C, D, and E together along the long edges in the order shown to make strip set 1. Press the seam allowances open. Sew one 4½" x 11" strip *each* of gray fabrics A, C, and D and one 2½" x 11" strip *each* of gray fabrics B and E together along the long edges in the order shown to make strip set 2. Press the seam allowances open. Crosscut *each* strip set into four segments, 2½" wide.

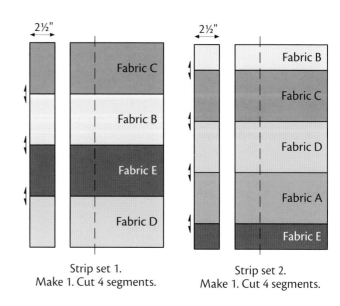

2½"

Fabric C
Fabric B
Fabric E
Fabric D

Strip set 1.
Make 1. Cut 4 segments.

2½"

Fabric B
Fabric C
Fabric D
Fabric A
Fabric E

Strip set 2.
Make 1. Cut 4 segments.

2. Alternately arrange the segments from both strip sets into eight rows, reversing every other row of the same strip set to create the pattern. Sew the rows together. Press the seam allowances open.

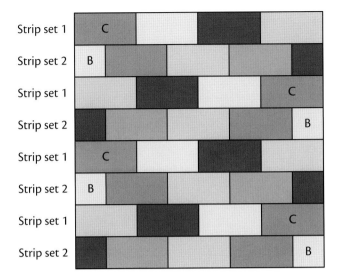

3. Refer to "Freezer-Paper Appliqué" (page 11) and use the appliqué patterns (page 76) to trace one each of patterns A–E and five of F onto the dull side of a piece of freezer paper and cut them out. Use the freezer-paper templates to prepare one of each A–E branch from the assorted brown fat quarters and/or scraps and five F leaves from the assorted rust fabrics. You will reuse the templates.

4. Referring to the branch placement guide (page 76) and the photo (page 70), position the branches on the pillow top, lapping pieces under others where shown. When you're happy with the placement, pin the pieces in place. Appliqué the pieces in place, removing the freezer-paper templates using method 1 before completely stitching around each piece. Repeat the process with the removed templates to make three more sets of branches from the remaining brown fabric and appliqué them to the pillow top. Because these branches represent nature, they don't have to all be positioned the same.

5. Randomly place the leaf squares across the pillow top and appliqué them in place, removing the freezer-paper template using method 1. Use the removed templates to prepare 10 additional leaves and appliqué them in place.

FINISHING THE PILLOW

Follow the instructions under "Pillow Construction" (page 14) to finish constructing the pillow.

Back to Nature

Try appliquéing a branch and some leaves on the pillow back, and use square buttons that mimic the leaf shape along the opening. Position the buttonholes different distances from the opening edge too.

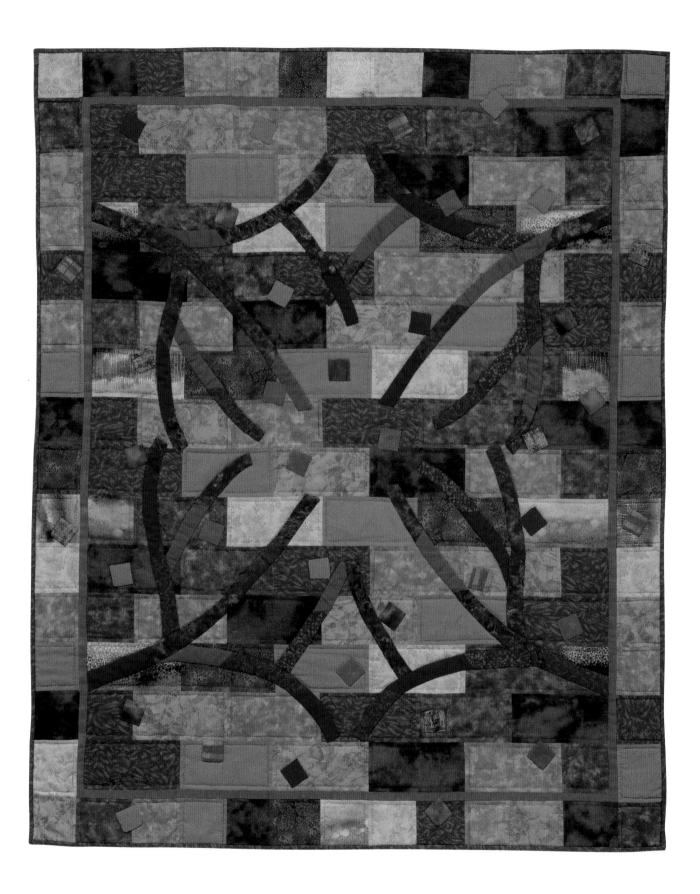

Wall Hanging

Assembling the Wall-Hanging Top

1. Sew one 6½" x 15" strip *each* of gray fabrics B–F and one 3½" x 15" A strip together along the long edges in the order shown to make strip set 3. Press the seam allowances open. Sew one 6½" x 15" strip *each* of gray fabrics A, C, D, E, and F and one 3½" x 15" B strip together along the long edges in the order shown to make strip set 4. Press the seam allowances open. Crosscut *each* strip set into four segments, 3½" wide.

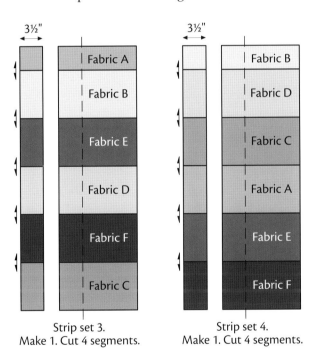

Strip set 3.
Make 1. Cut 4 segments.

Strip set 4.
Make 1. Cut 4 segments.

2. Repeat step 1 with the gray 6½" x 12" and 3½" x 12" strips to make strip sets 5 and 6 as shown. Crosscut each strip set into three segments, 3½" wide.

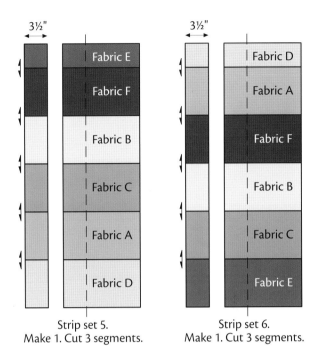

Strip set 5.
Make 1. Cut 3 segments.

Strip set 6.
Make 1. Cut 3 segments.

3. Arrange the segments from the four strip sets into 14 rows. Sew the rows together. Press the seam allowances open.

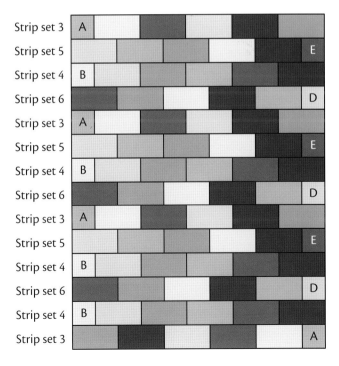

4. Refer to "Freezer-Paper Appliqué" (page 11) and use the appliqué patterns (pages 77 and 78) to trace one regular and one reversed each of branch patterns 1A–1D; 2A–2C; 3A and 3B; 4A and 4B; and 5A–5C onto the non-shiny side of a piece of freezer paper and cut them out. Also trace eight of square leaf pattern 6 and cut them out. Use the freezer-paper templates to prepare the branch pieces from the assorted brown fabrics and the leaf templates from the assorted rust fabrics. You will reuse the templates.

5. Referring to the patterns, stitch the pieces for each branch together, sewing just outside the edges of the freezer-paper template. Press the seam allowances open.

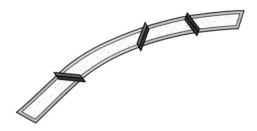

6. When all of the branch pieces have been joined, refer to the photo (page 72) and the piecing diagram below as guides to arrange the pieces on the wall-hanging top. The reversed branch should be positioned adjacent to the regular branch. When you're pleased with the arrangement, pin the pieces in place. Appliqué the edges in place, removing the freezer-paper templates using method 1. Use the removed templates to make one more set of regular and reversed branches and appliqué them in place.

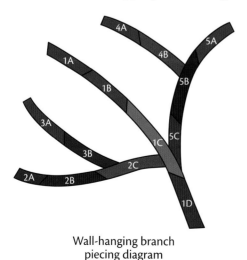

Wall-hanging branch
piecing diagram

7. Center and pin the rust 1" x 35" strips to the top and bottom edges of the wall-hanging top. Carefully sew in place, backstitching at the beginning and end. Press the seam allowances toward the rust strip. Cut off the excess ends even with the wall-hanging sides. Repeat to sew the rust 1" x 44" strips to the sides of the quilt.

8. To make the pieced outer borders, make strip sets 7–9 in the same manner as for the quilt center using the remaining gray 3½" x 7½" and 3½" x 15" strips. Crosscut the strip sets into the number of 3½"-wide segments indicated.

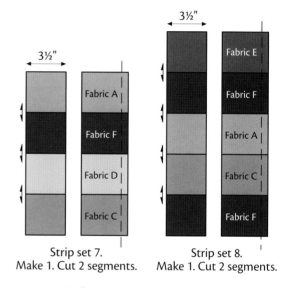

Strip set 7.
Make 1. Cut 2 segments.

Strip set 8.
Make 1. Cut 2 segments.

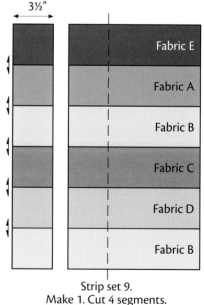

Strip set 9.
Make 1. Cut 4 segments.

9. For the top and bottom outer borders, sew one segment from strip set 7 and one segment from strip set 8 together end to end. Press the seam allowances open. For the side borders, join two segments from strip set 9; press the seam allowances open. Sew a gray 3½" x 4" rectangle to both ends of all four border strips. Add a gray 3½" square to both ends of each side border. Press the seam allowances open.

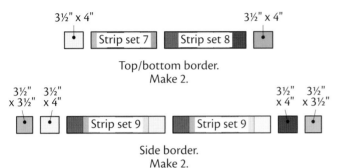

Top/bottom border.
Make 2.

Side border.
Make 2.

10. Center and pin the top and bottom pieced borders to the wall-hanging top and bottom edges. Carefully sew from one side to the other, keeping the seam line very straight. Press the seam allowances toward the rust inner border. Repeat to sew the side borders to the sides of the wall hanging.

11. Randomly position the leaf appliqués on the wall-hanging top and appliqué them in place, removing the freezer-paper templates using method 1. Use the removed templates to prepare 24 additional leaves and appliqué them in place.

FINISHING THE WALL HANGING

Refer to "Wall-Hanging Construction" (page 17).

1. Sew the gray fabric F 6" x 53" and 42" x 53" pieces together along the 53"-long edges to make the backing piece. Press the seam allowance open.

2. Layer the quilt top with batting and backing; baste the layers together.

3. Quilt as desired, referring to the photos (on the previous pages) for ideas.

4. The border for this quilt was cut oversized; after quilting, trim it to about 3" wide to square up the quilt.

5. Bind the quilt using the gray fabric F 1¾"-wide binding strips.

6. Add a hanging sleeve and label, if desired.

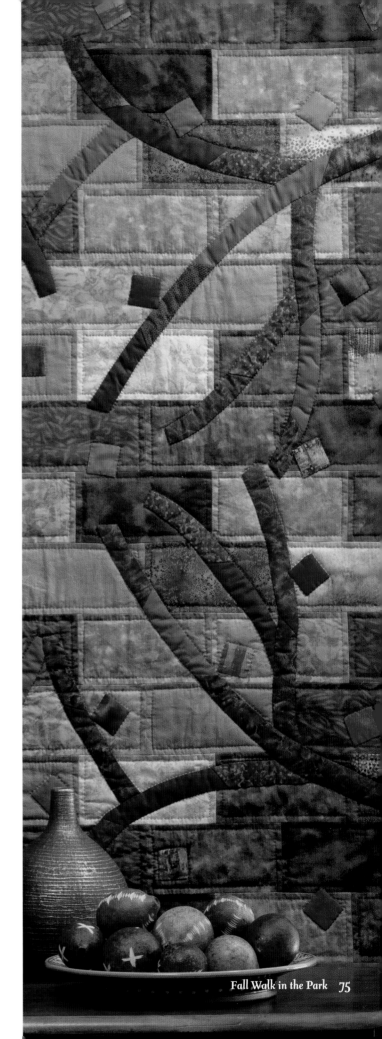

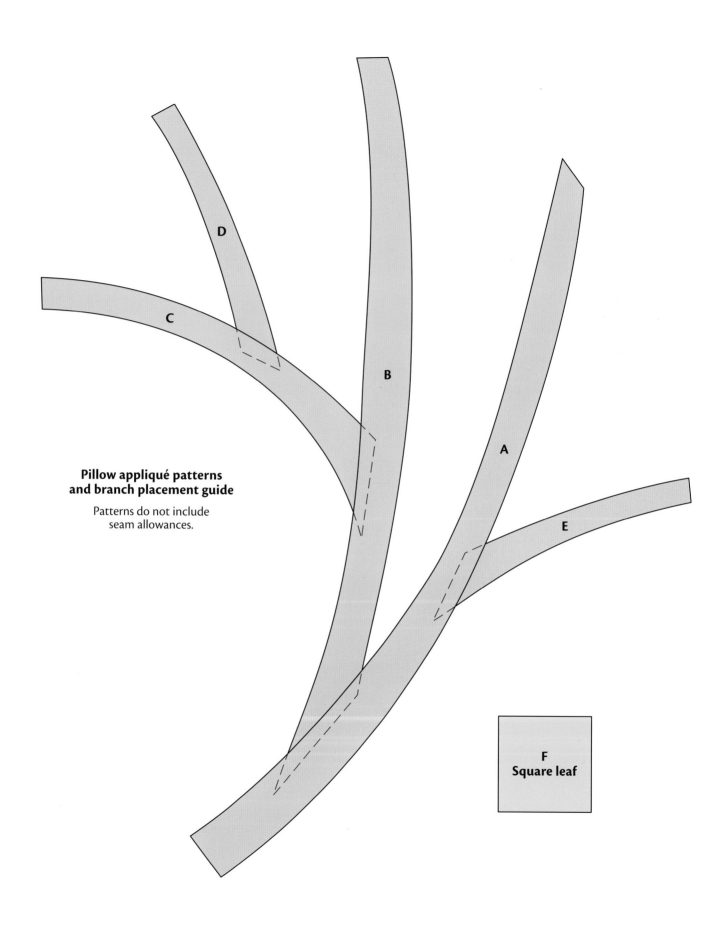

**Pillow appliqué patterns
and branch placement guide**

Patterns do not include
seam allowances.

D

C

B

A

E

**F
Square leaf**

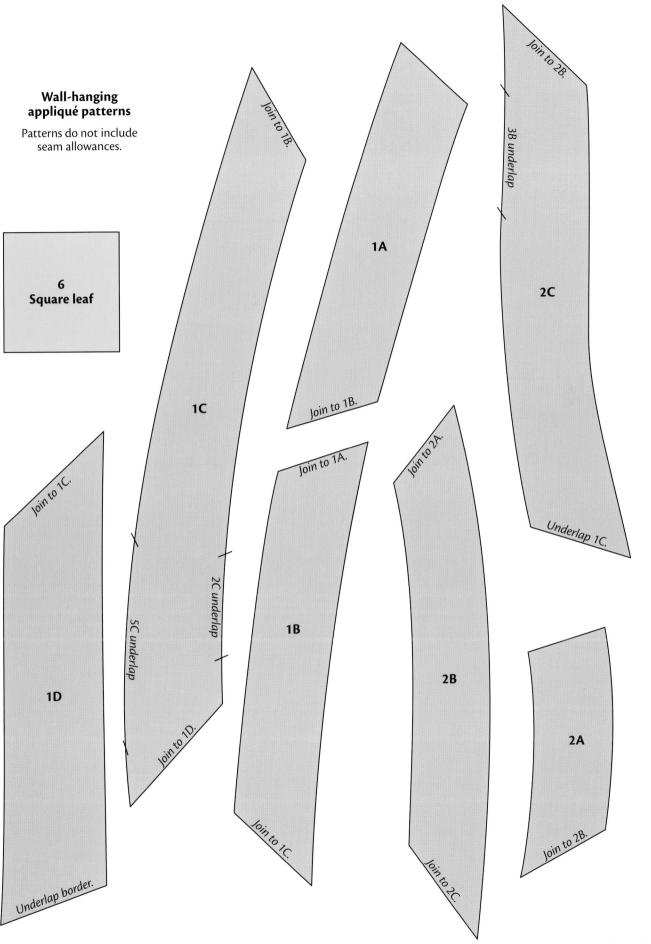

Wall-hanging appliqué patterns

Patterns do not include seam allowances.

6
Square leaf

1C

Join to 1B.

1A

Join to 1B.

Join to 2B.

3B underlap

2C

1D

Join to 1C.

5C underlap

2C underlap

Join to 1D.

1B

Join to 1A.

Join to 2A.

2B

Underlap 1C.

2A

Underlap border.

Join to 1C.

Join to 2C.

Join to 2B.

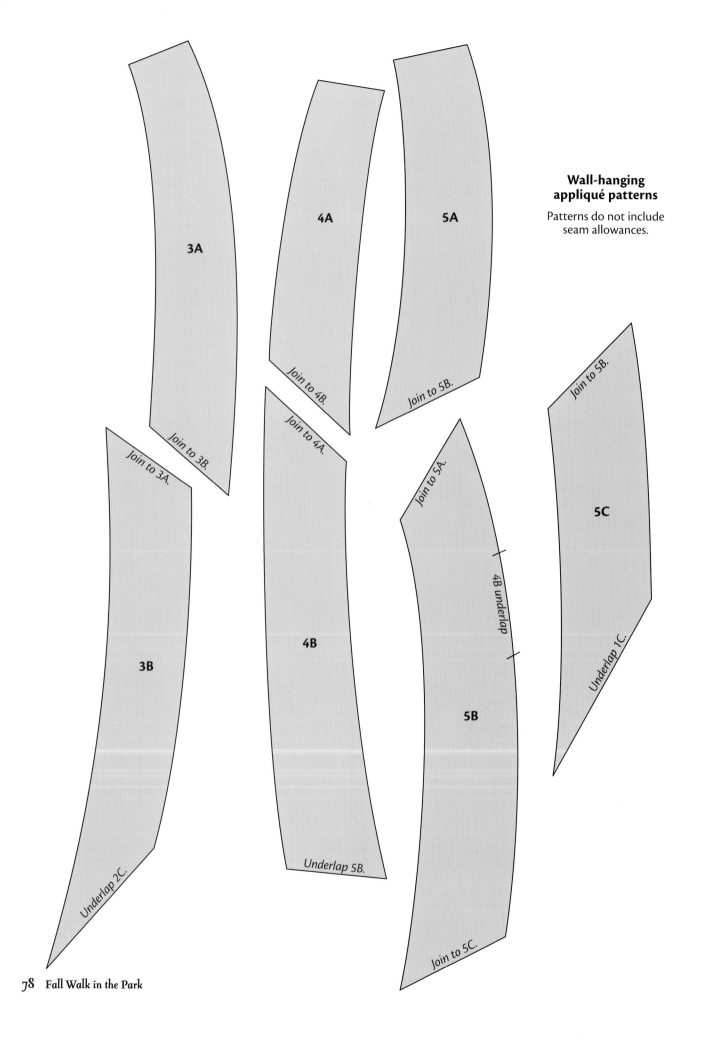

Wall-hanging appliqué patterns

Patterns do not include seam allowances.

3A

Join to 3B.

4A

Join to 4B.

5A

Join to 5B.

Join to 3A.

Join to 4A.

Join to 5A.

Join to 5B.

5C

4B underlap

3B

4B

5B

Underlap 1C.

Underlap 2C.

Underlap 5B.

Join to 5C.

About the Author

Sue grew up in the small town of Waxahachie, Texas. After college (at Texas A&M University), she moved to the big city of Houston, which turned out to be a great place to learn to quilt! Sue's mother got her started on this new passion one summer vacation, and the availability of so many quilting shops in Houston kept her going.

Sue and her husband relocated to Everett, Washington, where she joined a local quilt guild. She was constantly inspired by the many talented women in the Seattle area.

Since 2001, Sue has (mostly) enjoyed the challenges of living in Asia. In Singapore she was a member of two different quilt groups and in Japan was a member of Tokyo Friendship Quilters. Members of the groups were women from all over the world, so there were great opportunities to learn other cultures and how quilting is done in different ways. Sue also taught "American-style" quilting while living in Yokohama. Her students were fellow ex-pats and Japanese women. She learned as much from them as they did from her! China was next on the agenda, where the quilting challenge was having no quilt shops where Sue lived. She was really glad for her big fabric stash!

Sue and her husband have two daughters, Alyssa and Amanda, who are in college and high school.

There's More Online!

Find exciting books on quilting, sewing, knitting, crochet, and more at www.martingale-pub.com.

You might also enjoy these other fine titles from

Martingale & Company

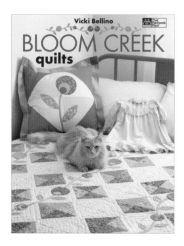

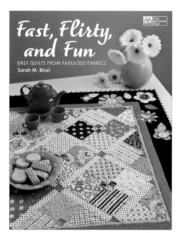

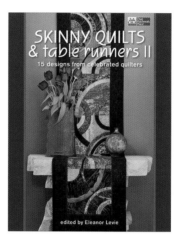

Our books are available at bookstores and your favorite craft, fabric, and yarn retailers.
Visit us at www.martingale-pub.com or contact us at:

1-800-426-3126

International: 1-425-483-3313
Fax: 1-425-486-7596
Email: info@martingale-pub.com

Martingale®
& C O M P A N Y

America's Best-Loved Craft & Hobby Books®
America's Best-Loved Knitting Books®

That Patchwork Place®

America's Best-Loved Quilt Books®